Because I Care

Because I Care

A Collection of Thoughts

X. W. Ng

PARTRIDGE

ISBN: Softcover   978-1-5437-4395-1
               eBook   978-1-5437-4394-4

Print information available on the last page.

To order additional copies of this book, contact
Toll Free 800 101 2657 (Singapore)
Toll Free 1 800 81 7340 (Malaysia)
orders.singapore@partridgepublishing.com

www.partridgepublishing.com/singapore

Contents

Preface

I will put it upfront that I apologize if I ruffle some feathers with what I've written in this book. Though backlash never feels comfortable, I would still write the same nonetheless, for there is nothing that means more to me than being genuine.

I started on this book in the spirit of wanting to express what has been buried inside me for probably too long, and in some ways to help release the guilt of having kept too silent on important topics that matter. Sharing about these topics, which are all very close to my heart, was my way of hopefully returning some justice to their significance.

Within the pages of this book, I freely share my world with you. To whoever out there who is reading this right now, I may not know you personally (yet) but I am greatly honored to have your attention for what I have got to say, even if just for a brief moment.

Above all, I just hope you enjoy the book.

"Love where love is lost, trust where faith is weak."

For

The Ones Who Hear My Song

About Me

Hello there, I'm X.W. Ng,
Just a few lines about myself here.
I'd confess upfront that I'm an oddball,
With constantly buzzing brain activities.
It is no wonder I barely sleep 3 hours a day.
Often, I feel like an old soul in a young body.
Yet I easily escalate into an 'adrenalized' mode,
Much like how a kid behaves when it is play time.
People usually can't read me, but I fully understand.
I have a deceptive appearance for what goes on inside.
In my free time, I enjoy all art; music, dance, you name it.
For songs I love, I literally play them on repeat for weeks.
Yes I'm crazy that way. At least, I'll remember the lyrics.
I love life in general, and strive to live for experiences.
Just simple things like feeling wind against my skin,
Or the aroma of fresh grass, fills me with such bliss.
This book is personal, yet I can't wait to share it.
It just intuitively feels like the right thing to do,
Because reading is simply, heaven on earth.
And if my book can pass on good vibes,
That would be my dream fulfilled.

thelovingpresence.com

facebook.com/xwng88

1

About Tenderness

"There is a price to be paid for every increase in consciousness. We cannot be more sensitive to pleasure without being more sensitive to pain." – British philosopher, Alan Watts

My dad and I share a habit of having nightly talks. An unspoken but mutually understood commitment to revisit our safe haven of bared souls and vulnerabilities. I will admit that this probably holds true more so for me than him. Nonetheless, the main point being, he represents my emotional safe house.

Nostalgic recounts of my childhood days came up recently, and we found ourselves poking fun at some of my idiosyncrasies as a kid. *"Your daughter is a very sensitive girl"*, my then kindergarten teacher always used to tell my dad. Singled out and labeled. My dad would smilingly acknowledge, fully understanding every word. After all, he's been that ever-present figure throughout some of my most fragile and tender moments.

When I was younger (perhaps still a little now), I struggled with being extremely sensitive. What does it mean to hyper-sensitive? Let me attempt to describe it to you. You feel surrounding energies deeply and you notice just about everything. You absorb moods in the room, non-verbal signals are deafening to you, you notice every nuance, and your senses are quickly inundated by the sights, smells and voices all around. Yes it is that intense. Feeling empathy becomes your status-quo modus operandi, a round-the-clock emotional reflex. Whenever you find yourself in a crowd or group, your heart naturally seeks out the weakest, most forgotten or vulnerable ones in the bunch. Being constantly this emotionally involved is not as easy as it sounds. Especially during my younger years (I am still rather young), being highly sensitive was not anything to be proud of, not even close. I learnt early not to expect to be understood. It was difficult to know, especially as a child, how this characteristic about you was not to be detested and ashamed of. From the outside looking in, it was difficult for others to grasp you, from the inside looking out, you would give up explaining. There lay an un-negotiable disparity of inner worlds, which would often mean resigning to your rightful corner where you understood deeply but was barely understood.

I love how poet Eric Hanson put in words, some of my exact sentiments on the complexities of attempting to understand another. He wrote about how there was no single key that led to the truth of one's being. He said of himself, *"I have the universe inside. Don't tell me that you know me. I am the universe in motion, for I was born from stars."*

A good few years have passed. How I see my sensitivity now, after years of wading in the mysteriousness of my own skin, is with a newfound fondness. Over time as you go along the flow of life, you begin to uncover the preciousness of your tenderest sides, where by 'side' I'm making an understatement. At least for me, it would be more like a big chunk of 'side'.

There is a certain kind of God-given brave that we are blessed with, in exchange for living a life with heightened sensories. It is not our choice to make how we're born to be, but if you are a certain way, trust that your form is an absolute necessity in ways you may or may not yet understand.

Keeping yourself together in the face of a seemingly jarring and careless world is pretty remarkable stuff. I can fully resonate with that. This kind of brave would feel something like a surge of energy, so formidable that diving headfirst into the hottest of messes with suffering and pain in sight actually feels intuitive. The urge to share someone else's emotions, especially their struggles, far overpowers the seeming comfort of observing from the sidelines, and far overshadows the tempting indulgence of ignorance and apathy. This may come across as just another sick form of masochism to some, to which I can only say is sadly misunderstood.

Philosopher John Rawls expressed in his magnum opus, "A Theory of Justice", that *each person possesses an inviolability founded on justice that even the welfare of society as a whole cannot override.* This is a powerful statement, which also happens to remind me about a recent episode of being chastised, albeit in jest, by one of my annoyingly adorable friends that being 'overly empathetic' on a personal level is at odds with the bigger picture of achieving greater good which should necessitate the sacrifice of a few. Unfortunately, I still can't make myself agree on that. I don't think sacrifices imposed on a few can ever be outweighed by the so-called greater benefit of majority, whatever the case may be. Human complexities don't function like Mathematics, they are neither formulaic nor clear-cut black-and-white. The way I see it, each individual is as valuable to his parents and loved ones as is the case for any other person, period.

Some of us don't see a few's sacrifices as worthy of batting an eyelid, for they claim that unsuccessful people deserve their fates as a result of their own doings. These people believe that a person's successes are most deserving and rightful since he was the one who made it all possible through individual effort, blood, sweat and all. While I don't deny that there is some truth to that, it is certainly not the whole truth. While one's superior qualities do pave the way for success, and with many of these qualities possibly acquired through one's own effort, there are always circumstantial factors and favorable inborn characteristics that are also at play in contributing to the overall recipe for success. We are quick to lay claim to our achievements, but also equally quick to bury our native endowments in oblivion - the God-given 'freebies' that made it that much easier a ride for us towards our goals and dreams.

It is with mindfulness that we should avoid making light of another's predicament. Those who suffer poorer fates than ours are not deserving of their misfortunes due to their lack of hard work or the like. For the most part, our starting points in life were pretty much handed to us and hugely disparate to begin with. We are far from being the sole creators and masters of our achievements, and our character and abilities have depended in large part on fortunate family and social circumstances for which we enjoyed a free pass on. As coined by Rawls as the 'veil of ignorance', imagine if you were not you, how would you want the world to be like? Keeping this question at the back of our minds does help shed some of our self-indulging thoughts.

For all those out there who like me have a heart too easily bruised, I hope we at least remain strongly wounded. May the intensity of our staggering emotions some day translate into energies so powerful that they lift all those around us whom we care so deeply care about. To borrow some words of wisdom from one of the ancient wise men, when asked which was the best city to live in, Solon, an Athenian lawmaker, replied *That city, in which those who are not wronged, no less than those who are wronged, exert themselves to punish the wrongdoers.*

2

About Love

I have personally benefited much learning from others' wisdoms and experiences. So it is my heartfelt belief that keeping quiet time to ourselves for reflections and reaffirmations of our core values is not only extremely important, but completely necessary. There's something to be learnt from everyone. Forget for a second about the traditional modes of formal education that we're all too familiar with. I believe much of learning exists beyond classrooms and textbooks. Life's true mentors come in various forms and exist in everyday encounters; they may be of any age or background. The only limitation preventing us from discovering and learning from these everyday mentors is often our ego, and by that I mean whether we can muster the humility to acknowledge these gems that exist all around us.

As humans, no one of us is perfect. When we exist as individuals, we naturally possess blind spots. However, the instant a few individuals are put together, there is a collective capability as one man's strength covers for another's weakness, and the unit as a whole becomes much less imperfect. I suppose this is also where the allure of the much-espoused teamwork lies.

Learning from someone else's experience can be extremely enlightening because of its first-hand nature. These accounts are often honest and real, exposing both sides of human nature - triumphs as well as vulnerabilities. The most inspiring stories are often exchanged with tears, sweat and at times, bloodshed. Learning from human experience is in fact a practice that respects human life itself; it is an act of doing justice to the emotions felt, the pain suffered and the sacrifices made in exchange for valuable life lessons. In respecting human experience, we value human life.

I find reading is one of the best ways to learn from another's experience at a deep and resonant level. We may not realize how extremely blessed we are today with such easy access to books and online writings. The convenience at which we can benefit so richly from those whom we are complete strangers to, is nothing short of miraculous every time I think about it. We are able to get our hands on content of superior quality, such as the essence of decade-long research studies conducted by renowned professionals, in the comfort of our own homes and without spending more than a few dollars on a book or close to nothing on an online article.

Like how American poet, Mary Ruefle expressed in one of her writings, *"In one sense, reading is a great waste of time. In another sense, it is a great extension of time, a way for one person to live a thousand and one lives in a single lifespan."* The marvel of reading not only lies in the download of content, but also in its meditative nature. Reading isn't a competition, it's not about how many books we devour in a day that matters. At least for me, it is always about the 'how' and 'why'. The beauty of reading lies in reading for reading's sake, with no element of urgency, and with the sole intent of interpreting and assimilating insights, inspiration and learning lessons fully and deeply.

When reading, one exists in a state of being where it is just you and you alone with a book, in peace and quiet. Ironically, reading can be described as a luxury due to its simplicity. When the mind is focused and our guards are down, we see things for what they are, sans veneers. Reading in this unfettered state of mind is akin to planting healthful seeds in our precious mind garden. Being mindful of our thoughts forms the basis of our spiritual health. In fact, spirituality has little to do with our external environment, it is more about the atmosphere we create within ourselves. It is not about becoming special, or becoming elevated to some celestial state, but simply about becoming one with everything. On the contrary, an unattended mind can create havoc because it is blindly receptive to anything that is fed to it. An unattended mind is dangerous, for it gradually forms your subconscious, which has the ability to influence your actions without your conscious agreement.

As lasting remarks to this chapter, I thought it would be good to share some of my key takeaways from past readings, with some of my own reflections thrown into the mix. I believe it is always worthwhile to spread notions of love and kindness, for these ideas resonate with all of us the same and reach the depths of our common human essence.

On Judgment and Compassionate Love:

❖ Never believe anything that anyone says. Always look at people the way they are, make your own conclusions about others based on your personal experiences with them. If we place greater emphasis on someone's past over their present selves, and believe hearsay more than our own direct interactions, we do not give justice to reality nor are we respecting truth as it should be presented, pure and unadulterated.

❖ When we judge others, we have no time to love them. Judgments prevent us from seeing the good that lies beyond appearances. We should always be mindful about serving others not because of who they are or what they can give us back in return, but simply because of who we are. If we can offer help from our hearts out of genuine compassion instead of obligation, then we are truly protecting the goodwill and dignity of our relationships.

❖ We should remember that we can never fully understand someone else's circumstance because we can never be them. With this understanding, we will begin to appreciate the courtesy of refraining from judgment, and simply seek to understand. Because simply put, nobody is perfect.

❖ There is a very fine line between good and evil, and it exists within all of us from celebrated elites to the average Joe. None of us is infallible to temptations, because that is human nature. It is with good reason that we should come from a place of compassion, as we seek to understand and empathize with those who have erred.

❖ At a deeper level, it is important to realize that individual material gains are transient. What is important is what we all share, such as notions of love, unity and togetherness. Our cultural narratives should promote these ideas. Sadly, many large corporations set out to exploit negative aspects of humanity for selfish and short-term gains. At times, society becomes so obsessed with shortcomings, it fails to recognize strengths and appreciate diversity in individuality. While I understand some of the more practical motivations for doing so, amidst an increasing strain on resources and egoistic needs to get ahead of competition, we must not overlook the lasting influence that negative societal forces have especially on the vulnerable minds of young children. If we cannot leave only the best for posterity, I think life is stripped of much of its meaning.

On Unconditional Love:

❖ The most terrible form of poverty is loneliness and the feeling of being unloved. When it is about giving love, there is no need for us to wait for a leader, or be told what to do. It is never wrong to love, if we do it, do it immediately and do it alone if we have to. Some of us get overwhelmed by the burden of how much we think we ought to give or contribute, so much so that we lose the big picture and give up trying altogether. If we can only manage helping one person at a time, then that is already better than inaction in all ways. "If you can't feed a hundred people, then feed just one", as Mother Teresa so aptly put. We can say life is as good as a fixed amount of time and energy. Putting this time and energy to maximum use to serve others will always be our one true North.

❖ Love exists in many forms. To me, unconditional love comes tops. Self-development and spiritual growth with the aim to better practice unconditional love is worthy as a lifelong personal project for anyone at any stage of life. Unconditional love goes beyond loving just your family or cultural groups, it sees no limits and it is abundantly given to everyone and anyone. It does not impose rules, selfish desires nor expectations. Unconditional love is simply about allowing someone else to be exactly the way they are without the need for them to fulfill us in any way. It has nothing to do with the quality of the receiver, but only to do with the character of the giver. I believe this love is the strongest force there could ever be, possessing the power to overcome the plague of fear and become a cure-all for any emotional or mental ill.

3

About Authenticity

"Life is the most difficult exam. Many people fail because they try to copy others, not realizing that everyone has a different exam paper."

Authenticity - this word holds much deeper meaning than the seeming simplicity of the word itself. Most of us associate it with the quality of being genuine and real, although much more than just 'being yourself' as the adage goes, it is more precisely about being yourself with finesse. Arising from an internal state of self-awareness and comfort with one's identity including all of one's past and present idiosyncrasies, being authentic means being consistent in word and deed, and having a strong fundamental character that shows through in unwavering fashion, regardless of the different roles and responsibilities that one may undertake.

Most of us hold authenticity in high regard, but similarly recognize the challenges of attaining it.

We are living in a generation that is so preoccupied with keeping up with the world that we rarely make time to find ourselves. It is scary to think that so many people die without knowing their true self, that which lies beyond their illusionary societal identity. It does not help that social media influences and cultural conditioning are increasingly designed with the intention to draw out negative aspects of human nature for quick commercial gains, making it that much easier for us to succumb to distractions and misguided notions. Social protocols and 'herd' mentalities run rampant, often clouding our view of our inner compass, and squeezing us dry of the strength and willpower needed to manifest our true selves. It is no wonder that it can therefore be such an uphill task to uphold our authentic identities, amidst all the chaos that surrounds us.

"Authenticity is not something we have or don't have. It is a practice, a conscious choice of how we want to live." – Brene Brown, author of "Rising Strong"

To me, the authentic self is a product of both intentional and attentive effort. With the complexities of modern day living and associated societal pressures and influences, it is not always intuitive or instinctive to be genuine, especially towards others. It takes specific commitment and conviction to take charge of this personal evolution of self towards the best version of itself, as decided by the individual. The authentic self therefore rarely occurs by chance, and takes considerable self-work and disciplined effort. An authentic self is by no means a mere perpetuation of the past self. If that was the case, I think it would actually be the worse version of self, for it would simply lead to a 'status quo' state of self that coasts along in mediocrity and which experiences no growth and improvement.

When one is being authentic, it should feel 'right'. It should fill one with a settling sense of ease and peace, where everything is in harmony and balance, and every action, word and thought is in perfect alignment with one's internal coordinates. As Adam Grant, author of "Originals: How Non-Conformists Move the World" described, authenticity requires closing the gap between your internal beliefs and external projections. This is in practice really much more complicated. In some ways, deceit makes our world go round, similar to the way white lies are founded, without lies, some marriages would crumble, some egos would be shattered, and governments would collapse. Ultimately, to be authentic or not is up to personal choice. It would be far from authentic if it were any less than a fully conscious and wholehearted decision.

I admit that when it comes to matters as personal as this, to each his own. As for me, I know with surety that if I did not find my bearings and serve out my authentic self, I was doomed to live a life unlived, a consequence too regretful to bear with.

As writer Victoria Erickson put it, *"Life is too short for pretend. Don't do things by halves as casual is a casualty, and time isn't renewable."* When given a choice, always choose real.

4

About Everyday People

John F. Kennedy famously said, *"We must find time to stop and thank the people who make a difference in our lives."* A good reminder indeed, of something that should at all times be kept at the back of our minds. Wherever we stand in life right now, we should not turn a blind eye to the fact that none of us got to where we are today without having received abundantly from the world around us.

We have received richly from our environment since the time we were born; from the air we breathe, to the food we eat and the unconditional love we receive from family and friends. We have been blessed with the possession of our bodies, a miraculous piece of machinery that handles the complexities of keeping us alive and functioning with such fluidity and finesse. Entering the world as a baby, we started in a most vulnerable and reliant state, with only needs and nothing of value to offer back in return. Yet, since our infant times, we have only benefited richly from the gifts of good fortune that had supported our fragile existence till this present moment.

However, as most of us grew into adulthood, we began to be caught up with the thrill of striving and achieving, and distracted by the pleasures of material comfort and worldly possessions. Ideas of self-sufficiency and other self-serving notions that placed undue importance on individualism quickly consumed our minds, and in worse cases, became central to our day-to-day thoughts and actions.

With the tendency of us humans to grow out of appreciation, especially upon acquiring greater freedom and independence as we mature in age, I decided that having a chapter dedicated to reminding myself of my humble roots that hopefully would nudge me into remembering to give thanks where it is due, would be both timely and worthwhile. Before we go too far into aggrandizing our individual ability and over-inflate the significance of individual effort, I thought it would be wise to consciously exercise some restraint over any awry tendencies, before they lead us too far astray from our primal and basic nature of love and compassion. More specifically in doing so, I wanted to make special mention of a particular group of people I call the 'everyday people'.

Thorton Wilder, American playwright and novelist reminded us that being alive is about the moments when our *"hearts are conscious of our treasures"*. Everyday people as I call them are the ones who we encounter most often in our day-to-day lives, and who may be people we may or may not be personally acquainted with. Nonetheless they are the ones whose hard work and contributions towards our well-being are most easily forgotten. These everyday people appear in our lives in various forms and inconspicuously too, from the shop assistant who meticulously prepares our daily meals to the bus driver who tirelessly takes us places in our daily commute. These unsung heroes, though unadorned with any ostensible wealth or status, have nonetheless collectively brought huge conveniences to our lives day in and day out, through their most heartfelt and miniature of ways. In fact, they have made things so comfortable for us that we easily miss taking notice of their efforts.

So let us remind each other to take a moment every so often, to remember and acknowledge the efforts of everyday people. While we may not always be able to reciprocate in big ways, simple gestures like a genuine smile, a friendly conversation, or just few words of appreciation, go far further than ignorance and indifference ever would.

The more calculative amongst us may perceive these everyday people as doing their 'rightful jobs', in defense of their reluctance in offering specific gratitude for their 'expected deeds'. To these people, I thought it would be worthwhile to point out the distinction between a job well done and doing the bare minimum. Over and above the bare transactional nature of a paid job, there is often a huge sprinkle of an intentional human touch that turns these jobs into kind acts of service that go beyond the call of duty.

If only we took time to notice beyond our own egos, we begin to discover the countless occasions where others go the extra mile for us at no expectation of reward or recognition back in return. Beyond what mere dollars and cents can measure, there is much more to us humans in our capacity to love and serve.

"Without the kindness of strangers you wouldn't have food on the table or a roof over your head." Being aware of this basic fact is the very first step we could all take to help spread and grow these positive facets of humanity.

5

About Identity

"Who am I, Why am I
Even body which was mine,
did not stand by my side;
I don't know,
Who am I, Why am I"
- extract from poem by Sadashivan Nair

I was pondering recently about the concept of personal identity. Not because I'm struggling from some existential crisis as some of you may immediately correlate to, but this thought just randomly found itself in my mind as I people-watched while having my routine sips of solitary beer.

The question looming in my mind was so simple you'd probably laugh hearing it, but what is identity? This question seems incredibly unimportant to get answered, yet, a nagging voice in my subconscious tries to suggest to me that it deserves some decent regard.

To expand on the question beyond what identity was fundamentally made of, I was curious and clueless about where our personal identities resided, whether within our physical form, or otherwise? Would you still feel like you if you lost an arm? The answer to most I believe, would be a straightforward yes.

So clearly, it appears that identity has nothing to do with our physical attributes, yet we pour alarming amounts of time and resources into our physical appearance, which quite effectively makes us feel a boost to our identities. The only way I could reconcile this difference would be the distinction between a false identity, which would then be associated with our physical aspects, and a true inner persona, which has to do with something much less tangible.

Further thought about this 'thing' called our true identity reveals something interesting. If we went through all our bodily parts questioning each's relationship with and contribution to our sense of self, it would occur to us eventually as we go about this exercise that our true identity is most intricately linked to one part of us more than any other, and that is the brain.

Our brain holds the key to all of our thoughts, our proclivities, our loves and our hates. The collective set of characteristic values we have play a major role in defining our identity. These characteristic beliefs in totality, form our 'intuition' and motivates our 'impulses'. The ability to understand something instinctively without the need for conscious reasoning, or the sudden strong urges we sometimes get in response to situations, are in fact the results of deeply-ingrained belief systems in our heads.

Beyond our beliefs alone, English philosopher John Locke expanded further on the concept of identity, where he surmised that personal identity was a matter of psychological continuity founded on consciousness. In this line of argument, he singled out memory as central to identity. He expressed that identity was marked by a personality that *"extends itself beyond present existence to what is past"*, where memory was the extension of consciousness to the past. It follows that our memory distinguishes from that of other persons, and it is therefore through the consciousness of memory that we remain the same person over time. As young artist and poet, Ming D. Liu expressed, *"I am made from all the people I've encountered; That is who I am."*

Of course, as with any opinion, there will be counter-opinions. John Locke has had his fair share of critics and counter-arguments which pertained to his philosophical views on identity. While I do not myself at this point, feel that I have ironed out these ideas enough to even attempt espousing any specific perspective, I do find it no less intriguing that this fundamental question about our identity and core existence can be so enlivened by the multiple dimensions that have been discussed. I believe this thought will continue to linger in my head for a while.

6

About Art

"Listen to the beat of your heart, listen to your art."

Throughout a large part of my hitherto tiny life, I've been pretty much buried in textbooks, those related to mathematics, science and all things geeky of course. My world had for a long time been an explosion of theories and facts, governed by precision and absolutes, and measured with technical exactness and balanced equations.

Having spent that long ravaging the world of scientific law and mathematical jargon, I must have at some point tipped some kind of internal scale when my view of the world subconsciously grew into a dangerously lop-sided one. Like an epiphany, this triggered a hot-headed and passionate foray into the world of arts, that parallel universe that I had barely dipped my toes into since I got a C for art and craft in primary school. This sudden change of heart was intense, to say the least. Nonetheless, I've enjoyed every bit of it and never looked back. It feels like I found my heaven on earth in art, this alternate universe that has been nothing short of a solid safety deposit for my most complicated and bizarre inner world. The interpretation of life in all its forms, couldn't be more succinctly expressed as Osho, an Indian spiritual teacher did, *"Make your life an aesthetic experience. Experience life in all possible ways - good-bad, bitter-sweet, dark-light, summer-winter. Move in all directions, be a wanderer."*

After I stumbled upon the universe of all things arty-farty, I discovered my whole-hearted devotion to its magic. Art - the true currency of an enriched life and a meaningful existence. Like how John Steinbeck, American author and winner of the 1962 Nobel Prize in Literature elegantly wrote, *"What good is the warmth of summer without the cold of winter to give it sweetness?"* What draws people to art? For me, it strikes right at our innate penchant for beauty, our enthusiasm for pretty things. Art embodies beauty, an honest kind of beauty embedded in the human spirit, in nature, and in movement and expression. Appreciation for the arts occurs to me as the lowest common denominator that universally connects all souls. From a simple blooming tulip, to the vast oceans and skies, all of the beauty that nature presents can't quite be as perfectly preserved and expressed as in pieces of carefully crafted art. This universal language of beauty in artistic expression is one that we all speak.

"Industry without art is brutality. Art is nothing tangible. The thing made is a work of art made by art, but not itself art. The art remains in the artist and is the knowledge by which things are made." - Ananda Coomaraswamy, pioneering historian and philosopher of Indian art

Art however, is so often portrayed as some sort of eye candy, or an esoteric extra. Only when you have personally applied brushstrokes of your own emotion, and created your private painting upon the canvas of your own reality, will you understand how art is very much a necessity. Like medicine, it provides a shot of therapy and carries an emblem of hope for weary souls. To Pablo Picasso, *"art washes away from the soul the dust of everyday life"*. This couldn't be more true. It is easier now than before to slip into the material trap of the modern day, where worthiness is linked to price tags like second nature. Art brings us back to a heartfelt evaluation of worthiness, through appreciation of intrinsic value in its purest form. I adore how art reminds us of beauty in the simplest everyday things we so easily take for granted. The clouds, the beautiful morning sun, and the night sky, all of nature's endowments bestowed upon us for free and in such abundance. When we cast aside the plain commercial value of things, and discover real value through an honest and personal experience, we may sometimes return beauty to its rightful place and shed light on its often-neglected worthiness, hidden in the seemingly mundane. Art offers a much-needed respite from our frenetic consumerism and protects us from soul-devouring commercial exploitations. I love how art brings justice back to the depths of humanity and returns honor to our primal virtues of reading in between the lines, interpreting the unspoken and ultimately, staying true to our inner compasses.

Art isn't just pure beauty, it is courage. Art forms like literature and philosophy often valiantly stand opposed to dominant value systems that reward status and wealth. Through the power of language, written works bring out human experiences in all honesty, complete with their fair share of trials and tribulations. Our common struggles and vulnerabilities, when expressed through art, ironically bring out our most redeeming and unifying virtues. With simplicity and elegance, art reminds us of the normality of pain, in the way a somber piece of art provokes the realization that there is nothing embarrassing about experiencing suffering. Art seeks to connect us to one another through our common miseries, and assures us that we may find solace in these moments of weakness which are simply part and parcel of the human condition. Above all, art returns us to our authentic selves by teaching us to look past veneers of false optimism carelessly painted before us.

I take my hat off to artists. The best ones express so perfectly what we ourselves can only feel but are unable to articulate. They possess this bizarre ability of knowing more about us than we do, despite not actually knowing too much about us. They are able to jolt our thoughts through their artistic magic, gently yet powerfully reminding us about the big questions - the deep and important questions that often get brushed off as superfluous yet hold key to guiding our biggest priorities in life and directing our most precious energies for a meaningful existence.

More personally, art helps tame my wildfire spirit. It provides that much-needed counterbalance amidst the daily cacophony that goes on in my head. My chaotic mind finds a safe haven in art. Somewhat ironically, there is a special serenity I feel in its boundlessness. When art speaks to you, it feels like the warmest embrace in a cozy place where there is limitless capacity for the forgotten, the neglected, and the rejected. Art carries a passion for truth and honesty, with all imperfections, gray areas and vulnerabilities in tow.

Art is also where creativity finds its rightful home, for me, a place where I both find and lose myself. Art keeps my hyperactive sensories occupied, offering both release and indulgence. From a heartfelt piece of prose, to uplifting music or a mesmerizing sequence of dance, art encapsulates the best of visuals, textures, movement and flows of energies, like no other.

"Your art is not about how many people like your work, your art is about whether your heart likes your work. You must never trade honesty for relatability." - Rupi Kaur, Canadian poet and author of "Milk and Honcy"

What's there not to love about art really? Just talking about it fills me with much excitement and euphoria. It instantly breathes life right to the soul. I often wonder how we could make art better flourish, or help propagate its many embedded wisdoms and spread its doses of spiritual richness. In what form, and in what way should we best institutionalize something so fluid, dynamic and rather mischievously elusive?

I reckon I'll leave these thoughts lingering for another day. As art taught me, good things take time.

7

About Courage

"I wanted you to see what real courage is, instead of getting the idea that courage is a man with a gun in his hand. It's when you know you're licked before you begin but you begin anyway and you see it through no matter what."- Harper Lee, To Kill A Mockingbird

I recall with fondness, this quote from one of the compulsory readings for literature class back in the day. This recollection is a rare one, for not much of what I learnt in school has remained in this bird brain of mine.

Today feels so much like the perfect day to talk about courage. Don't ask me why, for when my intuition tells me so, I dare not question. I have to admit that for a characteristic as majestic as courage, any amount of writing couldn't do it justice, so pardon my irreverence if I fail to accord it the gravitas it so deserves. The notion of courage is intriguing. Most of us may not be aware that the Latin root of the word actually means "heart", so to live with courage is in fact to live with heart - heart as opposed to head.

I have these somewhat odd moments when I feel proud to be human, especially when I witness how something as powerful as courage is demonstrated within human capacity. Courage underpins almost all positive action - courage in love, in overcoming odds, in losing personal pride and ego, in communicating with honesty and integrity, and the list goes on. In fact it may be difficult to identify otherwise. To live with courage is in a nutshell, about choosing to be alive. It is about living in insecurity, being at ease with the unknown and unfamiliar, and to march forward despite full knowledge of impending difficulties, possible danger and risks. Indian spiritual teacher, Osho, described courage as having a heart that is always ready to take a risk. *"The heart is a gambler. The head is a business man. The head always calculates – it is cunning. The heart is non-calculating."*

I've read stories of the most awe-inspiring displays of courage, by people who have absolutely no logical reason to be courageous, as the head would rationalize. Courage shows itself in all forms, from a soldier risking his life on the battlefield, to standing up against authority to protect dignity and virtue, and to making personal sacrifices in exchange for another's liberation. I often wonder how people become courageous in the first place? Just as commanding as courage is, the lack of it is an equally powerful contagion. What makes some people rise up from the crowd and voluntarily take on gigantic risks when it makes their lives so difficult? This seems even more bizarre when nothing material is guaranteed in return.

As with most things unfortunately, doing good the hard way is most often the rarity rather than the norm. From my own brief dabble in the corporate world, I have been (pardon my insolence) most sickened by the overwhelming majority who have fallen to the dark side, and blatantly taken the most cowardly of routes. The fear-mongering and gossip just seem to enjoy a life of immortality, even going from strength to strength in a vicious cycle that appears impossible to escape. To be fair, the majority's mentality can be understood. Widespread 'ego inflation' and the subtle downplaying of the individual's capacity to bring about change, have made any form of resistance against establishment or going against the flow, extremely discomforting for most rational minds.

But really, what's at stake is by far greater. The loss of human spirit is a greater tragedy in every sense of the word. The strength of a lonely conviction against the ills of systems and cultures, and the integrity of rising above hatred, apathy and selfish pleasures for a clear conscience, are truest displays of the unadulterated essence of being human. Take for example the most common practice of gossip, any amount of self-serving benefit gained through rumor-mongering could never justify tearing someone else down. Too often, we underestimate the power of a kind word. It is much harder to repair a broken person, than to build someone up. If we see ourselves as connected to each other and all but part of a larger human family, then when one does good and feels good, we do better and feel better collectively.

I'm still an adamant believer of the innate goodness in all of us. I believe we are all kind at heart, and that we all similarly desire to lead a good life, defined as one that brings joy to those whom we cross paths with. But we do get quite easily overwhelmed, distracted and easily led away from our moral compass. Being ignorant may be convenient, but protecting our values and the integrity of our thoughts define our lives. The line between good and evil lies within every human heart, it is neither defined by race, religion nor social status. We are all as infallible as each other, as human as each other. Celebrating or condemning another is similarly meaningless, for we all bear the same potential to be kind and loving, and likewise, bear the same risks for erring on our weaknesses.

Courage is like a muscle, the more we use it, the stronger it gets, and the less we train this muscle, the more incapable we become at flexing it. Let us resolve to practicing some courage each day, just a little a day and we shall together triumph over all darkness.

8

About Independent Thought

Have you ever wondered, when was the last time you had an original thought? By this, I mean a truly original idea borne out of an innate untainted response towards something you have personally observed and experienced first-hand. A response charged with individual pursuit, be it out of passion, love or concern for another, and devoid of externally enforced controls, agendas, or cultural expectations.

The idea of self-reliant thinking, or more specifically, making your own conclusions, is more elusive than it seems. This is often the case with many grandiose ideas - easier said than done. We may be less independent in thought than we think we are, and much lazier in practice than we wish to admit.

"Our danger is that equality may mean training for all and education for none," said C.S. Lewis. He cautioned against a generation that acquired great knowledge of the world yet understood little about great literature, where education was outshone by training and civilization dies.

Because I Care

Let me first confess that I struggle with the concept of independent thought myself as well. Sometimes I even think it takes a superhuman of a being, to persist with that rugged individualism, especially in the face of what seems like a tsunami of cultural pressures and social forces that permeate all aspects of our lives, through the power centers of media, language, systems, and instruction.

During my brief stint in the corporate world, I had managed to earn myself enough infamy to be labeled some sort of rebel or 'rough around the edges' as they called it. Sometimes these were told to me in jest, and other times, they were suggestive of somewhat more serious undertones. Fortunately for me, being typecast an oddball isn't a new life event and naturally didn't bother me.

What people seldom understood was that I derive no gratification in sticking out like a sore thumb. While I admit that there are some people out there who compulsively challenge general opinion out of a more self-serving desire to simply draw attention to themselves, not all who come across as different from the crowd bear such motivations. What many may not appreciate are the often-hidden struggles of resisting pressures to conform in the spirit of guarding one's convictions. Whether a blessing or curse, I happen to be the sort of person who would rather die true to my beliefs and values, than gain immortality living life on someone else's terms. This may sound extremely logical on paper, but is strangely uncommon in practice.

Napoleon famously spoke about the world's suffering, as a consequence not so much from the *"violence of the bad people, but because of the silence of good people."* I think this quote isn't well remembered for no good reason. Most of us are not unfamiliar with the inner voices constantly played out in our minds, the devilish ones that almost always succeed in coercing us into blind submission. Uncertainty, doubt, and the fear of knowing too much, often make it all too easy for many of us to play ignorant. Other times, we succumb to exhaustion from an overload of mundane daily affairs so much so that we slip into a pathetic state of apathy and sloth. Some of us would have come across expositions on the power of habit, quite a trendy topic in recent self-help books. And it is often the case that the positives of habit are portrayed. But just as powerful as good habits are, unhealthful habits borne out of ignorant compliance are dangerous. What we think about becomes our reality, and if we do not think, we are literally not living.

"It is the mark of an educated mind to entertain a thought without accepting it" said Aristotle. If there was just one thing we should never live without, it would have to be to own our mind. All of our actions are preceded by our thoughts. The moment we outsource our thinking, we have lost our very essence.

In the current climate of information overload and stifling societal instruction, it has admittedly become a great challenge to remain curious, and to be brave enough to act on our curiosity. Yet despite the struggles, our integrity is always worth reclaiming at whatever cost. Our personal identities are worth much more than the limits thrust upon us, and our responsibility to personally observe, investigate, and guard against fallacies, is a far greater cause than any level of blind conformity.

Taking in life's lessons is akin to reading a good book, as how Malik S Muhammamd expressed in his book, "Think Big, Grow Big, In Business and In Life!", all that any book does is to awaken the reader to possibilities. The wisdom of a good book can only be received if it was met with a genuine willingness to experience that intelligence. As he rightly said, *"You may teach a person from now until doom's day, but that person will only know what he learns himself. You can lead him to the fountain, but you can't make him drink."*

9

About Productivity

Most of us have at some point or another in our lives, been unwillingly dragged into some sort of 'rat race', or forced by circumstance into conforming blindly to senseless protocols. In the area of work, we are not unfamiliar with archaic rules, outdated methods, and forbidding red tape. Day-to-day must-dos that we know clearly in our guts to be irrational are often so rampantly thrust upon us like sacred edicts.

I am sure the mere mention of all this would draw some sympathetic nods as we recognize these common frustrations that hit us all the same. The way I see it, two types of people come out of such circumstances, the first being the office drone who decides that sacrificing his soul would be the lesser evil, and hence becomes resigned to being led by the nose, and the second being the notorious rebel, who upon being pushed past tipping point, is jolted into action and creates massive upheavals everywhere in his path.

Our insatiable greed to squeeze out more 'productive outcomes' from our already-stretched waking hours has turned into a large-scale obsession. In the workplace, we are inundated by overwhelming loads of meaningless yet tedious tasks, and increasingly find ourselves at the beck and call of incessant and unnecessary requests. What has productivity come to today?

Select Your Work

Famous author of best-selling book, "The 7 Habits of Highly Effective People", Stephen Covey highlighted the distinction between prioritizing our schedules and scheduling our priorities. This notion does indeed make us wonder how our cultural and corporate narratives stack up to what productivity is truly about.

If we put aside our egoistic need to glorify an over packed schedule and boast about our perennial 'busy' status, can we still convince ourselves, in all honesty, that we are creating meaning out of each passing minute and making the most of our time and attention? This question is not as trivial as it may seem, for it is those small minutes that become days, which then become years, and eventually form our entire life. When we take a moment to pause and reflect, we can often quite easily reconnect back with our purpose, as the bigger picture tends to present itself clearly and simply if we are willing to see it.

Being productive shouldn't be difficult, in fact it couldn't be more logical that we should seek to attain that. But before we even go there, we need to first and foremost, "know thyself", for if we are not familiar with the person whom we're dealing with, i.e. ourselves, we will naturally be unable to make the most of our own selves.

Humans are not robots, and this self-awareness takes work. Self-knowledge takes a kind of inner work that only we ourselves can undertake and in fact, it is a personal responsibility that we should regard with importance. We must seek to understand thoroughly the nature of our being, including all intricate nuances of this custom machinery. We must be mindful that we are the vehicle to deliver results for all our endeavors, and this vehicle can only be optimized as well as it is understood.

Self-knowledge involves a solid grasp of how we perform best, including how our energies vary throughout the day, which is the best time for what type of work to be undertaken, where our interests and strengths lie, and even when we need to rest our minds and recharge our souls.

Conserve Your Energy

Most of us today, have become too easily led by pre-determined schedules and instructed tasks that are all too often so poorly designed that they only scrape the surface of our greater potentials. Let us take the example of the typical 9 to 5 workday, though so widely practiced and accepted, this continuous block style of work is in fact so suboptimal in terms of matching with our natural rhythms for producing good work.

Assume you are an artist engaged in creative work. I would not expect you to produce your best work after dutifully ploughing through an 8-hour block. Or say you were a scientist working in the lab, I would similarly not expect you to consistently perform at highly specialized tasks with complete clear-headedness throughout those consecutive hours. You get the idea. While I do not intend to generalize here, I would say that most of our work do not take kindly to such an illogical work arrangement. Our mental capacities and energy are a limited resource, and sorry to be a wet blanket but this basic fact holds true no matter how mentally strong or energetic one may be. Research has even gone as far as to tell us with some precision that our attention spans average around 30 minutes to an hour. So it is really an intentional false optimism that we continue to 'believe' in our ability to sustain a continuous stream of ingenious ideas and excellent work over unreasonably long hours. If quality of work was what we were truly after, as opposed to clocking hours for a workday, then we are clearly off-target.

Other than optimizing how we work, it is just as important to think about what we are working with. Or to put it simply, what actually needs to be done?

It is admittedly a challenge to remain steadfast on this when piles of work are constantly thrown at us. But to be fair to ourselves, we must always stay committed to filtering out clutter and keeping a focused eye on greater objectives. If we really pared down each task to its core purpose, and actively questioned its contribution towards desired end goals, we will often find that initially perceived work volumes can be reduced by shocking extents. We are often quick to spring into action, but much less disciplined about taking a moment to think before acting.

While I understand the tempting comfort of just getting things done, even if the task was silly or utterly extraneous, we should be mindful that the time spent doing something is indirectly taken away from doing something else which could possibly be more worthy of our attention. Efficiency is mindless talk if the task at hand was in the first place, unnecessary.

Work Smart

Other than a clever choice of task, we could go further to noticing even subtler nuances, such as how we can achieve the most with the least amount of time and resource. This is outlined well by the Pareto principle, or 80/20 rule which describes the phenomenon of minority contributions giving rise to majority effects.

Some of the most productive people are astute at picking 'the path of least resistance'. That familiar maxim about how you will achieve anything you want if you worked hard enough, I'd suggest taking with a pinch of salt. In this modern time, working smart cannot be understated. Sure you can work hard for a lifetime, but only if you are comfortable with the fact that someone else can reach the same endpoint in a day or two. Working smart is more about conserving our own precious time and energy, than just something convenient to brag about.

Avoid Senseless Multi-Tasking

Thinking back to my stint in a corporate environment, I recall being extremely repulsed by the over-glamorization of the so-called 'multi-tasker'. That senseless race to be crowned the busiest person with the most on his plate. This trend was rather prevalent and spoke volumes about how some of us were so desperately in need of justifying our billable hours. The reasons for this desperation are obvious and probably don't require my further elaboration. The fact of the matter is that our brains are wired to focus on one thing at a time. Most managers honestly do not respect this basic human physiology.

If two tasks were involved, the only way we could engage in both simultaneously would be if at least one of the tasks was so well-learned that it had entered our subconscious and required negligible focus or thought in doing. Another possibility would be that the two tasks engaged different areas of the brain. Sad to say, in most of our work, we would have barely reached that 10,000-hour 'rule of thumb' mark to achieve the said subconscious ability, and further to that, our job functions are typically too complex to strictly stick to distinctly isolated processing centers of the brain.

Beneath the guise of multi-tasking, what we are effectively doing is highly-distracted serial tasking, where we hop from one task to another in rapid succession, spending more time than ever to complete all tasks, as opposed to focusing on completing one task at a time expeditiously.

Remain Flexible

Finally, after we have made all the right moves and gotten ourselves a neat little plan, just remember to avoid the trap of falling too much in love with your plan. Pre-empt change and be truly comfortable with that. Even the most perfect-looking plan can't escape minor tweaks and refinements along the way once the action starts.

The wisest workers are able to reach that fine balance between spending sufficient effort devising a sound plan and avoiding holding on too tightly to the plan. It is worth remembering that no matter how much preparation is done, there is no real feedback to what we have considered until we start doing. As Leonardo Da Vinci put it, *"Knowing is not enough, we must apply"*.

True learning occurs through doing, and experiencing a few hiccups along the way is more than normal. So be willing and open to change, and just as important as that is to be forgiving of yourself if your plan didn't turn out as perfect as you imagined.

Final Thoughts

With all that is said, the point is that we do not always have to move mountains to do incredibly awesome stuff. It is completely possible and within our means to make fast and simple approaches work for the most intractable situations or complex problems. The key lies in a willingness to give careful thought before action. Whenever we are thinking, nothing can go too wrong. So if I had to tell you just one last thing before I end off, it would be to never stop thinking, because your true value lies in your mind.

10

About Small Talk

I felt this topic could do with a chapter on its own, deceptively titled 'small talk" but is in fact more about the art of making friends.

I recently came across an interesting word. *"Kargauer"*, a German last name of an excellent family. Often thought as smarter, stronger, and better than other people, Kargauers are known to have the ability to befriend anyone. Their charming looks and outgoing personality make people naturally want to obey them. Kargauers are also said to succeed at everything they do, and failure is never an option for them. Sure sounds like perfection, nobody wouldn't love to be a Kargauer anytime. What struck me most from the whole host of superior qualities was the ability to befriend anyone, which to me, is what truly sets apart those who merely survive from those who thrive in life.

It is not difficult to see the appeal of connecting with others and excitement of turning an acquaintance into a new friend. Every friend we have today started off as a complete stranger to us, and something as basic as an honest conversation can often lead us to the most soul-deep and electrifying connection. As the saying goes, *"Distance doesn't separate people, silence does."*

Small talk is indeed the new deep. Fortunately, all of us are made to be great conversationalists for the mere fact that every person is himself a really good book, carrying life stories that would unfailingly make for riveting conversation. We are at our core, similar in our human ways, in having desires and aspirations, and our share of emotions and vulnerabilities. Surrounding influences may sometimes distract us from this fact by conditioning us into casting labels and categories on people. Sadly, these distinctions often end up numbing our innate empathic capacities to identify with and feel sympathy for each other.

An honest, no-strings-attached conversation helps bring back our commonalities and teases out our grandiose ambitions and deepest desires that so similarly bind us. As Oscar Wilde said, *"Ultimately, the bond of all companionship, whether in marriage or in friendship, is conversation"*. At the heart of good conversation is kindness, courage, and honesty. Kindness in the choice of words and tone of language, courage in revealing our rawest parts, and honesty in sharing our thoughts and dreams, loves and hates. This may sound like a mouthful, but having deep and authentic conversations ironically comes with surprising ease. The simplicity of which lies in the natural flow of communicating without force nor coercion, unbound by expectation nor obligation, and freely welcoming of any topic from our proudest moments to our most embarrassing failures.

To quote a poem that very much captures the essence of a deep conversation, *"I want the words you are afraid to say - the lonely ones you keep hidden in between the folds of your heart."*

11

About Existentialism

It may not seem befitting to some of you that I foray into the topic of existentialism, especially so for a duckling like me amongst most of you old birds out there. Admittedly, my relative small age and much possible naiveté may barely give justice to the profundity of this topic, one of the strongholds of 20th century philosophy. Nonetheless, I couldn't curb that itch to unload my infantile mutterings, as always.

What first lured me into pondering about this idea more deeply, the notion of 'highest human potential' or *arête* as the Greeks so elegantly termed it, was when I stumbled upon a piece of ancient wisdom from none other than Socrates. *"I desire only to known the truth, and to live as well as I can, and to the utmost of my power"* - a statement seemingly innocuous, yet subliminally unintuitive and surprisingly consequential in practice.

Jean-Paul Sartre, a seminal French philosopher most known for his pioneering work on existentialism, couldn't have articulated more eloquently as he expressed existentialism as a fundamental humanism, where we are all but architects of our destinies. *"Life has no meaning a priori. It is up to you to give it a meaning, and value is nothing but the meaning that you choose"*. Whenever

I come across words like that, I can't help but pause to marvel at the remarkable beauty of language. The way language is able to send such penetrating shots of insight despite the brevity of words employed. The power of language in clarifying the depths of our souls is quite unmatched. Like Shakespeare said, *"The forms of things unknown, the poet's pen. Turns them to shapes and gives to airy nothing."* I apologize for the digression.

The concept of existentialism and highest human potential leads to discussions about taking on life with the highest level of personal responsibility and claiming full control of our choices, thereby becoming the best versions of ourselves. In other words, it is about the idea of reaching our ultimate potential. Far from sounding remote or foreign, these ideas are in fact commonly paraded maxims. However, as straightforward as they appear on surface, probing further into the actual practice of existentialism often uncovers a greater realm of intricacies, complexities and ambiguities, to say the least.

What does it take to be truly free and to genuinely live for yourself? I think it takes some pretty fierce resolve to be a master practitioner of this. We find ourselves thrust into this world and born into our circumstances, often more mired in cultural provincialism than we wish to be. Existentialists speak of how existence precedes essence, where we create ourselves through what we do as we become the sole artists of our lives, and in so being, we are free.

More often than not however, mustering the kind of stoicism to rise above the lies we tell ourselves eludes us. How does a basic humanism become so humanly impossible? Turns out that a common problem that plagues us all is something called *'mauvaise foi'* or bad faith. Most of us are, unfortunately, easy victims of self-deceit because avoidance of short-term pain is almost always too enticing to resist. It is more bearable to bury the thought of long-term impoverishment, and to tolerate slow (albeit prolonged) decay. Bad faith permeates our everyday life, from work to relationships. We tell ourselves that we suffer a scarcity of options, and we become pressured to draw a tight circle around our lives, closing off opportunities to expand our sights and minds. All this in exchange for the comfort of claiming that whatever happens to us is preordained and a destiny that one should rightfully surrender to.

To be fair, facing existentialism head-on is terrifying. Acknowledging that no ultimate authority exists, and that we hold full personal responsibility in creating our essence, is both liberating and anxiety-inducing at the same time. It boils down to a conscious decision to enter into an abyss of infinite uncertainties and unsettling unknowns. The desire to flourish and achieve *arête* unavoidably creates distress. However, this state of being is also ironically, one of the most predictable aspects about life. The reality of life is as Danish philosopher Soren Kierkegaard expressed, *"do it or don't do it – you will regret both"*.

However unpalatable this human condition, blindsiding it would simply be just another act of bad faith. Life has no predefined logic and everything is scarily possible. Choices are almost invariably ours to make. Whether we ride with the fluidity of existence, or box ourselves in under status quo and tradition, we will not escape having to face agony, in one way or another. Such is life. As for me, living life forwards would always be the lesser evil. If I had to connect the dots on hindsight, it still beats wasting precious moments regretting missed opportunities or past events.

12

About Engagement

I wanted to revisit an increasingly hard-to-seek experience
in the frenzied world we live in today, an experience so
prized and yet doesn't cost a penny, so deeply fulfilling
but often glossed over. I'm talking about the experience
of being 'in the zone'.

Many of us have heard of or even loosely alluded to this
phrase ourselves before. As for me, I've always been
somewhat hazy about its origins. The notion of being 'in the
zone' was studied and developed by renowned Hungarian
psychologist Mihaly Csikszentmihalyi (I'm glad this isn't
an audiobook and I save myself the embarrassment of
mutilating such a beauty of a name). In Mihaly's seminal
work, "Flow: The Psychology of Optimal Experience",
Csikszentmihalyi surmised that we reach the peak of our
enjoyment when in a fully immersive mental state with
the task at hand. He outlined that in this so-called state
of flow, we become so absorbed and highly focused that
self-consciousness vanishes and nothing else matters.
Under such intense and completely focused attention, the
experience becomes so enjoyable that one would keep at
the task regardless of its difficulties and even if at great
cost, for the sheer sake of doing it.

The idea of being thoroughly engaged and fully involved in a singular task, has become such a rarity in the modern workplace. This appears to be especially so now than ever before. When was the last time you recall yourself being 'in the zone'? To quote late comedian George Carlin, *"most people work just hard enough not to get fired and get paid just enough money not to quit"*. Recent surveys have shown that close to three quarters of employees are disengaged at work, and this number is only expected to rise. To be fair, it is not unrealistic that we make certain compromises on our private longings and other talents when we become specialized in very specific tasks required by the modern economy. The way work is organized in most corporations today follows the long-established practice of division of labor, where each of our roles functions as a tiny cog in a giant machine that optimizes collective efficiency and productivity. However, this practice also leads to a somewhat unnaturally enforced daily routine of keeping at the same task over substantially long hours. While we serve as specialists, I believe most of us are at heart, happier as generalists. American poet Walt Whitman expressed in one of his most notable works, "Song of Myself" that *"I am large, I contain multitudes"*. It is therefore no surprise that restlessness lurks within us more often than we think, and some degree of disengagement at our typical 9 to 5 jobs is more prevalent than we might imagine.

The above said, I remain quite optimistic about the possibility of preserving engagement despite the specialization of roles. In fact, at the other extreme, with some tenacity and in the right frame of mind, specialized work can be deeply engaging. One of the preconditions of experiencing 'flow' is to be distraction-free. Yes tell me about it. We are all but unwitting victims of the unabashed attention-robbers of modern life.

Most of us, at some point in our lives, have carried the guilt of succumbing to the crutch of social media. We are admittedly pretty powerless when faced with the onslaught of eye-catching advertisements, interactive web interfaces, and incessant flashes of the latest media gossip and pop culture news. There would be no other way to justify the millions of dollars poured into purposeful design of media platforms to draw us into a dopamine-inducing vicious cycle of reliance on social media. However, the detriments of this attention-robbing are becoming ever more felt, especially as we attempt to stay engaged in our supposed mainstay vocations.

The antidote to being dragged blindly into a degenerate state of cursory reading, hurried thinking, and thoughtless knee-jerk reactions can only be a greater innate awareness and premeditated discipline. As Csikszentmihalyi aptly put, control over consciousness is not just a cognitive skill. At least as much as intelligence, it requires the commitment of emotion and will. Someone who has achieved control over his energy and has invested it in consciously chosen goals cannot help but grow into a more complex being. Attention, is like energy in that without it no work can be done, and in doing work it is dissipated. We create ourselves by how we use this energy. In John Medina's best-selling book "Brain Rules", he revealed that studies have shown that a person who is interrupted takes 50 percent longer to accomplish a task. To make matters worse, he or she makes up to 50 percent more errors.

The reality is we do not have the luxury of infinite time to do infinite things. To reclaim control of our attention requires us to tap into our willpower. Yet willpower itself is not an infinite resource. In fact, the more we use it, the less of it we have left for subsequent actions. Like a muscle, willpower suffers atrophy with lack of use. While we may will ourselves into practicing self-discipline and focus at our tasks, respecting how our bodies work and understanding how our energies behave should still take precedence.

For some of us, difficult tasks tend to drain less willpower when they are repeated sufficiently such that they turn into habits that operate with relative ease in our subconscious. For some others who get more easily distracted by peer pressure or external temptations, the habit of proactively anticipating scenarios and preplanning responses often helps guard against being swept away by those forbidding forces. Of course, if only things were that simple.

Beyond the individual's own power to guard his attention and focus, there are stronger cultural forces that loom large. With the aggressive and often-exaggerated style of modern marketing, falling prey to a poorly-designed job seems to be increasingly the norm rather than the exception. We wade blind in a sea of mundane, low-value work masquerading as their diametric opposites in the job marketplace. These jobs are designed primarily to help the company succeed, often at the blatant expense of the success of the individuals doing the work. The false sense of scarcity created by the mass market of shallow work on offer in turn exacerbates our resigned outlooks, and fuels a downward spiral sacrificing the individual's success.

How many of us can proclaim with conscience that our jobs engage us in meaningful deep work, especially for the large percentage of us lying at the base of the corporate pyramid? By the looks of how speed has become so unabashedly favored in the modern rat race, the once-extolled exacting standards and unwavering insistence on quality all too easily slide into neglect. The kind of deep work that promises long-term success is unfortunately losing the battle against its more inferior sibling - shallow work that shore up instant gratification derived from a false sense of accomplishment.

To look on the brighter side however, there are ways to rise above those forces determined to drag us down. Knowing what we're dealing with solves half the problem.

One of the key tenets of flow psychology is the ability to create for ourselves, situations that induce flow. Inducing flow comes down to a neat balance between the level of skill and the size of the challenge at hand. When the challenge far outweighs one's skills, anxiety and stress ensue, which renders the situation unsustainable. Conversely, if the level of skill eclipses the difficulty of the task, distractions become easy temptations. To arrive at a state of flow, one must be wise in choosing compatible tasks, and that to me, is what 'job fit' is really about.

It has been studied that some personalities are genetically blessed to better perform at deep work than others. The term used to describe these blessed beings is 'autotelic', and they are people who are intrinsically motivated to perform tasks for their own sake, rather than to fulfill socially prescribed cultural stereotypes or hanker after extrinsic rewards.

If you find yourself not exactly blessed with the genes for being autotelic, the silver lining is that we are able to free ourselves from our genetic code through conscious awareness and self-discipline. Lucky for us, one of the redeeming qualities about being human is our ability to make choices that liberate us from being encaged by our inherent biologies. In fact I don't think any great work in human history came out from sitting back and allowing ourselves to be purely led by our genetics. And all effort will eventually be well surpassed by the rewards of engaging in deep work, which are undeniably and genuinely fulfilling and lasting. Austrian psychologist and Holocaust survivor, Viktor Frankl, illustrated this point remarkably in one of his most considerable works, "Man's Search for Meaning", where he explained that the crux of mental health stems from a certain degree of tension, *"the tension between what one has already achieved and what one still ought to accomplish"*. He writes that what a man actually needs is not a tensionless state but rather the striving and struggling for a worthwhile goal, a freely chosen task. Coasting along stress-free, having plentiful cash at your disposal and being lavished with extravagant gifts, are nothing but false pleasure. In reality, a tensionless state results in nothing more than an existential vacuum, as barren as the Kerguelen Islands.

At the end of the day, what we're all after is that long-lasting sense of happiness and fulfillment. It isn't so much about the actual achievement itself than how we feel about the kind of person we choose to be. Whether our efforts eventually lead to material achievement is somewhat secondary to the soul-filling contentment of striving to become the best versions of ourselves, and the joyful conscience of knowing that what we are creating and contributing is of real value to the world and done to the best of our abilities.

13

About Tolerance

I was indulging in some solitude the other day. Especially timely as those oompa-loompa thoughts of mine desperately needed some sorting out before they crowded out my tiny brain. Amidst that hazy entangled mess up there, I was hit by a spur-of-moment temptation to invite some company (a move I regretted later). Before the rational part of me could react to my moment of impulse, the next thing I knew was a friend was on his way.

Given his uncannily rich life experience peppered with quite the whole spectrum of trials and tribulations, I bore the expectant hope that perhaps his two cents' worth would contribute some clarifying wisdom towards my otherwise lonesome contemplation. Boy did I return home with a more convoluted mind than I started. And yes you probably guessed it, that evening spent with my friend set the premise of this piece.

Instead of two cents' worth, I received what seemed more like a jarring earful, a barrage of should's and should not's interspersed with a pelting down of moralistic censuring. I was too drained to react, and on hindsight, that was probably a good thing. I simply lay sat, silently attentive to not so much the contents of his words, but how they were expressed.

Just one question boggled me the whole time as he inundated me with his words of wisdom, said with gusto and certainty - how do we know if anything we know is true? More specifically, what I wondered about was where we derive our moral convictions and if it is at all possible for anyone to ever have all the answers for as long as we remain fundamentally human - imperfect and limited in knowledge, experience and our physical sense of the world?

Assuming we recognize and accept our innate fallibility and inherent inadequacies, then we may admit that we can never be all-knowing. And if that was the case, then when is one's advice ever valid to another? What all this led me to was the conclusion that the only surviving outlook should be one based on humility and tolerance.

Humility itself as an attitude, has never experienced enduring adulation. Its quality as a virtue has experienced its fair share of doubts, and its practice has been a substantially controversial one. A humble demeanor to some, stems from a submission to one's basic powerlessness. It creates some kind of tension, antagonistic with the more-revered notion of "self-esteem". Modesty has before, suffered the label as a sign of weakness and so has tolerance, which is still sometimes construed as just another form of moral cowardice. Well, I beg to differ.

G.K. Chesterton, the 'prince of paradox' and prolific English writer and philosopher put it most succinctly "*It is always the secure who are humble*". I tend to think true humility has been colossally misrepresented, and even at times sickeningly twisted by those attempting to conceal their individual failings at mastering this mother of all virtues. Nothing beautiful asks for attention. Where is the weakness in admitting that you don't do all things perfectly, and in staying teachable regardless of how much you already know? Where is the cowardice in not needing to be noticed, in walking with the broken and struggling? It is in fact, only the strongest of men who are able to accept humiliation and hurt with grace, who can remain kind and gentle under provocation, and who ultimately *"never stand on [their] dignity; to choose always the hardest"*, to quote one of the kindest people humankind has ever seen, none other than the much-adored Mother Teresa.

The idea of humility and tolerance usually leads to a libertarian worldview, where in its purest form, embodies absolute exclusion of bigotry in all its forms. Practicing tolerance is far from a bed of roses. In fact, it would not be a cause for concern nor worthy of public debate if not for its particular importance at times of controversy. The crux of tolerance lies not in the willingness to accept difference, but more in acceptance despite one's own discomfort or disapproval with that difference.

Libertarians steadfastly believe that it is never justifiable to use force against peaceful people, as everyone should have the right to do what they wish with their body and property for as long as they are not initiating force on another. This does not mean there has to be agreement with another's actions all the time, but it does encourage persuasion instead of any use of force or coercion at times of disagreement.

Audre Lorde, social theorist and poet, shed some enlightening insight in one of her essays, where she wrote that in a culture where good was defined by profit rather than human need, there exist people who are made *"to feel surplus, to occupy the place of the dehumanized inferior"* through designed oppression. *"Institutionalized rejection of difference is an absolute necessity in a profit economy which needs outsiders as surplus people."* And sadly enough, an unfortunate outcome of this is a society conditioned to respond to differences with fear and hatred. I do subscribe to the notion that one of the hallmarks of a truly liberal and civilized society is how well it practices *"live and let live"*, where each individual is free to be the master of his own ship, make decisions about his own life, and define the meaning of his existence on his own terms.

British philosopher Bertrand Russell brought attention to the notion of individual surety, which does help frame humility and tolerance in an interesting manner, as he surmised *"we ought always to entertain our opinions with some measure of doubt. I shouldn't wish people dogmatically to believe any philosophy, not even mine"*. Another notable libertarian of more recent times, Dr Milton Freidman, believed that philosophical doctrines that people claim to base their views were fundamentally a source of intolerance. How can we be sure if one was right and the other was wrong? How can we have absolute certainty about that which defines moral vis-à-vis sin?

In his first novel, "Nausea" published in 1938, existentialist philosopher Jean-Paul Sartre expressed his acute observation that the world was much more unfathomable than we think, much more queer and mysterious than we choose to admit. In his view, day-to-day routine was simply a predictability that we impose upon ourselves, a comforting logic that we ascribe to life. Sartre argued that the world reveals itself as highly absurd. Everything is terrifying possible, impossibly weird, and follows no preordained logic. This Sartrean perspective is fundamentally refreshing in that it strips our existence to its core, paring down all the prejudices and stabilizing assumptions that we so comfortably lean on.

Along the same vein, early Christian theologian and philosopher Saint Augustine underscored the weakness of men against their destinies. Augustinian pessimism in essence, theorized that the odds are stacked against us humans from the outset. Our lives are awry to begin with, not by coincidence but by definition, and all that we do as humans, fall within the bounds of imperfection.

We may have gotten used to holding ourselves mercilessly to stern ideals of so-called 'success' in life, this being further bolstered by inflated optimism and deceptive ideologies perpetuated by the media and other misleading cultural narratives. The false ideals of that perfect path in life, starting from a well-regarded formal education and landing a job we so love, to meeting a perfectly compatible partner and having a lovely family, and finally entering old age in graceful retirement with minimal ill-health and suffering. How many of us actually secretly hold ourselves to such impossible expectations, despite knowing how statistically rare this combination of scenarios was in reality? The world is in fact a much more uncertain and dangerous place than we want to believe, a place where undeserving suffering and unexpected deaths happen more often than we hear about, where we sometimes have to bury babies and young parents. We either don't at all grasp how rare and strange it actually was to steer clear of mishaps and disasters in life, or we have simply chosen to be wholly ignorant.

Despite the gloomy slant of the Augustinean view, the very point raised about the inherent flaw of the human condition in fact bears a deeply reassuring effect. We may ironically find solace in the generosity of this perspective towards personal defeats and failings of society. Personally, I find these ideas may at times be unsettling on first pass, but always manages to make one feel uplifted upon deeper thought. The latter is especially felt when one is undergoing some kind of struggle from the stranglehold of societal factions – each so deeply entrenched and imposing in their self-righteous prescriptions of rights and wrongs. In an Augustinean world, greater tolerance could retain its foothold on the basis of the 'original sin' of mankind. Forgiveness could be more generously dispensed to those unwittingly mired in earthly failures. The humility in recognizing the fragility and limitations of human reasoning and understanding provides a comfortable safe house, a retreat from judging each other by external markers of success and self-imposed moral standards.

Humility and tolerance should still have its place. The next time we find ourselves entrusted the role of confidante and listening ear to a friend in need, perhaps it would be worth treading carefully as we speak, all the time remaining fully conscious that we do not know the truth about the truth we know to be true.

Like how my favorite poet Nikita Gill puts it, *"Remember how vast the ocean's boundaries are. Whilst somewhere the water is calm, in another place in the very same ocean, there is a colossal storm."* Everyone carries with them a silent struggle in their own way, and everyone is fully entitled to that, without judgment.

14

About Women

Finishing this chapter won't be easy. On the bright side, at least you won't see me as I'm writing this and witness the hot mess I get myself into. As these thoughts and words flow out of me, I'm unwittingly reminded of some of the tenderer moments of my past – the crash-and-burn's that feel fresh again. Nonetheless, I harbor a glimmer of hope that other than satisfying the selfish desire to unload my niggling thoughts onto innocent readers, my soul-baring could perhaps provide some kind of warmth to those who find themselves in similarly rickety situations. This piece goes out to all my 'non-biological sisters' out there, especially those trying to pick up broken shards of their tender hearts. Let no one who stumble across this chapter leave it feeling more alone than they started.

I quote a piece from the "Wild Women Creed" by Pam Reinke, since good things are worth sharing and it conveys my sentiments in words much more put together than I could ever manage. *"Wild Women make it happen, gathering to celebrate the secrets of a sisterspirit, seeking to live life with volume and verve"*. There is much mystery about us women, as many men would agree in unison. To be honest, sometimes even I could neither comprehend nor explain. But I am sure about one thing, somewhere within that baffling strangeness lies incredible beauty.

This might sound weird coming from me, but in a completely non-narcissistic way, I confess my hopeless adoration and respect for women, in general. I've lost count of the number of times I've been utterly floored by the grit and grace of some truly awe-inspiring women I've had the privilege to meet. These are the women who have personified courage in vulnerability, and who are literally forged from searing flame. Only when you truly understand what being a woman is like and feels like, you would not sufficiently grasp the vast essence of being innately feminine, nor would you understand the depth of some of the silent struggles - those that embody a steely nature so deceptively masked by a mild veneer of humility, kindness and grace.

Women, all of them out there, are actually hopelessly soft-hearted creatures - knowingly and willingly so. The unique language of love they speak, perhaps sometimes laughed off as nothing more than weakness or naiveté, is ironically one of the most deeply cogitated choices made from a place of amazing strength and compassion.

Unconditional love to me, is the most endangered thing on this planet today, residing only in hearts as big as the infinite skies – a rarity indeed, but thankfully yet to be extinct. Like angels trapped in human bodies, women carrying such capacity for love overwhelm all those around them, while exuding an inexplicable aura of soothing comfort and warmth. I have in my personal encounters, been blessed and inspired by women who have exemplified strength in fragility. As hardwired nurturers and caretakers, these women touch everyone who crosses their paths, from their own children and family, to friends and lovers. In fact, I believe that the connection between and among women will always be the most potentially transforming force on the planet. And that is also why I think that women, unlike any other specie, will always be needed.

I have met some remarkable women, many of whom have touched me straight to the core. I'm not only referring to my own mother or mothers of my own friends, but the whole sisterhood consisting of generations of mothers and grandmothers to all others. Regardless of age and background, you find a certain purity in most of them. It exists in that unwavering conviction to keep immense struggles so deeply private, so much so that they are preserved in nobility and seek nothing of shallow validation nor contrived pity.

Women In Painful Relationships

I came to discover that often the most fiercely loving and giving ones have gone through difficult relationships with partners that bring with them troubled histories. While outsiders often pass judgment on this as a foolish act of self-sabotage, I think it is much-maligned. There are always times when people around us attempt to convince us about how well they know us, from the few facts they gather about us which they piece together in ways they deem fit. Therein lies the danger if one was not self-aware, for you may start believing their versions of you, which may well be nowhere close to the truth of your being.

The way these women seem to attract broken souls and their desire to 'repair' them are far from a sign of weakness and self-loathing, but instead a display of true strength and assuredness. Misconceptions arise when ignorant by-passers fail to comprehend the notion of unadulterated love. Humans tend to understand only from their level of perception, and easily forget the cruelty of judging that which we do not understand.

There is a difference between thinking of yourself less and thinking less of yourself. Love is sometimes about giving someone the power to destroy you, but trusting them not to. Strong people excel at being independent, and have invariably done much inner work to become so extraordinarily equipped to handle the pain and emotions of those who need healing, support and comfort. I believe that is why the universe somehow brings together some of the strongest people with the most broken souls, even if there was no active seeking out of each other. Reality is far from the ugly picture painted by skeptics - those who try to rationalize such beautiful unions as twisted attempts by weak-minded women to feed voids of self-esteem.

In partial defense of the women so often entangled in painful relationships and misunderstood by almost everyone else on their intentions, I feel the urge to expose their hidden gems and break down all assumed falsehoods. The truth is that only the immeasurably open and forgiving ones are capable of accepting anyone and everyone with an embrace so inviting and welcoming that only few can comprehend. Yes some women have an odd propensity to attract broken souls, but by no means is this in the way commonly labeled as 'self-victimizing'. Instead, it is out of a purity of love that there is a desire to heal and bring calm to the unsettled. In stark contrast to the pitiful image often painted, many of these big personalities are in fact quietly confident and spiritually grounded. Their silent contributions may be overlooked, forgotten or mislabeled, but there is no denying that these unsung heroes (or heroines to be precise) do much to lift spirits and elevate humanity. Like how poet Nikita Gill described in one of her writings, such angels *"love until fractured places become crevices, and the crevices become thin, white scars that [the broken ones] only just barely remember."*

Of course, humans are not perfect. The strongest amongst us are allowed to feel drained sometimes, from the immense work of healing others. We should be able to cut them some slack for their resolve and courage to never love by halves, but only completely, in wildfire ways. Relationships are expected to teach us the most about ourselves, even when we are already strong characters ourselves. The merging of two individuals is nothing anyone can anticipate or prepare for in full. I have myself had my fair share of heartbreaks and moments of crippling weakness, despite being a self-proclaimed passably independent person. Although I do confess that my problems are mostly self-inflicted - a consequence of holding myself to military standards of love that my emotions could barely manage. Indeed, sometimes being up close to people is just too dangerous, much like the flames you loved as a child that brought the fire that taught you pain.

Final Thoughts

If you are a woman reading this right now, and currently toughing out your own lonely struggle, I hope this little piece of writing could at least offer some slight comfort. A paragraph from one of Nikita Gill's poems never fails to calm me down at times of need, and I share it here in hopes that it serves you the same, *"The ghosts of all the women you used to be are all so proud of who you have become, storm child made of wild and flame."* So hang in there, my love.

15

About Food

I'm not sure why I'm admitting this, but as I write this, I'm also sheepishly stuffing my face silly. Come to think of it, I'm always eating. I just love food too much and am forever hungry. Naturally, I had to dedicate a full chapter to ramble on about one of my greatest loves of all time – food.

"Cooking is like love. It should be entered into with abandon or not at all," quipped Harriet Van Horne, popular newspaper columnist and film critic. To say I am obsessed about food and cooking is an understatement. Given any idle time, my mind easily wanders into a magical world of all things culinary, from wild thoughts about aromas and flavors to breathtaking masterpieces of plating art. In my mind's eye, I see floating tomatoes, sprinkles of fresh basil and dazzling displays of incredible Itamae-style knife skills. I like to joke that if I had my own home, all I needed would be a kitchen. The way my soul fires up and my heart palpitates whenever I walk into a spanking kitchen, that inexplicable surge of energy as my fingers glide over the smooth finish of an iron skillet, and the intoxicating feeling as my lungs take in wafts of wood emanating from the countertop, are all but a mystery even

to myself. And believe you have probably by now grasped the craziness of my obsession with food and cooking.

Food is something I often see as one of the most overlooked stars in our lives. Food keeps us going day in and day out in the humblest of ways, yet is rarely appreciated by most of us as we scurry along the humdrum routine of breakfast, lunch and dinner. The much-endeared Indian yogi, Sadhguru, returned some respect and significance to food, as he expressed it to be *"the single most important input to our bodies that transformed us from our mini forms as babies to what we are now"*. How resoundingly true indeed. Food, even as basic as bread and butter, gets absorbed into our bodies and eventually forms part of our physical form, which we all know to be a piece of miraculously-sophisticated machinery that keeps us functioning in inexplicably complex ways. The human body, together with all its innate intelligence, has unfailingly kept us going, despite the unforgiving demands of living we place on it. It is no wonder that food should deserve its due respect. Our bodies are sacred, and so does the food that feed it. As some chefs put it, we should always *"respect the ingredient"*.

Alex Atala, Brazilian chef and owner of the renowned restaurant D.O.M. in Sao Paulo is one of my all-time inspirations. Not simply a chef extraodinaire, his outlook on life, personal convictions and many noble missions often bring tears to my eyes. He embodies many of the values I hold dear, and more than that, his actual living practice of those very values touches me in very special ways. Even though we aren't personally acquainted with each other, and furthermore exist oceans apart coming from quite dissimilar backgrounds, having the chance to read about his life stories and learn about his work through the wonders of the internet, is already to me enough of an honor to behold a lifetime.

Through Chef Atala's perspectives, I am much enlightened about aspects of food and cooking beyond the kitchen itself. Food encompasses way more than what we might think, it is about a larger circle of life. There is a greater relationship that food has with nature, and food chains extend further upstream than commonly thought, all the way to local farmers and indigenous growers. Chef Atala brought to my awareness, the simple yet resounding fact that *"behind every dish, there is death"*. This may sound uncomfortable to some of you, but its truth is undeniable. It is in fact necessary to be constantly conscious of this fact, to better appreciate the life that was taken in exchange for our nourishment. This awareness gives us a sort of sensibility, to respect life and the natural environment.

Food preparation is more than just a plain process of turning raw food into cooked meals. Eating is more than simply fulfilling our caloric requirements. Every great chef I have come across carries an incredible passion for ingredients, is obsessed about how food is prepared, and strives for perfection in bringing out meaningful messages and evoking emotion through creative fusions of flavors. Their attention to detail is more deliberate than spontaneous. Food, when prepared with heart, sends incredibly powerful statements. They may contain hints of shared memories or speckles of long-held traditions. Little nuggets of wisdom about our cultures and the natural environment may lay hidden in a seemingly innocuous dish, only revealing its depths upon active discovery and appreciation. This is the reason I believe cooking will always retain its place as a respectable profession, in every sense of the word. For cooking epitomizes that special human touch that will always preserve and showcase our unique individualism.

The much-endeared chef and TV personality, Julia Child, famously said, *"The only real stumbling block is fear of failure. In cooking, you've got to have a what-the-hell attitude."* This may sound tongue-in-cheek, but is actually astoundingly accurate. The very process of creating great food is an exhilarating ride to say the least, and only through doing will you reach the pinnacle. You may be a decent cook, but you could never be an excellent one if you did not genuinely carry an open mind in the vast universe of cuisines and ingredients. A great chef also embodies the courage to experiment with tastes and a discipline for exacting execution. Most of us are able to tell if a dish is tasty or not, but only a few are acutely cognizant of the subtler underlying elements that ingeniously mesh together in delivering that satisfying sensation on our palates. The ability to achieve this successful fusion is nothing short of true art. Perhaps that's why people term it *'the culinary arts'*.

Cooking is not just about chemistry, or precise measurements and timing. Cooking also demands intuition and instinct as almost always, something will go 'wrong' along the way. It is in fact the personal adjustments made to a recipe that largely define the personality of the final dish. This is probably why the same recipe given to two individuals very often produces vastly different results.

Because I Care

Cooking is more an art than a mechanical process, and only the very skilled are able to showcase intriguingly mind-blowing styles on a plate. As expressed by Thomas Keller, chef and owner of landmark Napa Valley restaurant The French Laundry, *"a recipe has no soul, you as the cook must bring soul to the recipe."*

Despite the uniqueness that every great chef brings, you will still find a unifying hunger for challenge, a similar impassioned drive to step out of what is familiar and 'safe'. The best restaurants are also often the ones you never find standard menus. Instead, you are more likely to find yourself trying something you have never heard before, or perhaps didn't even know was edible in the first place.

A great chef is not only himself a mould breaker, but also challenges his diners to shed their cultural attachments and experience new flavors and novel ingredients. The mark of an accomplished chef lies in his ability to stretch minds beyond conventional definitions of fine cuisine and good food. Much like the interplay between risk and reward, what makes us uncomfortable often leaves us thrilled at the same time. Chef Atala often attempts to break down long-held societal conceptions about fine dining. He successfully demonstrates through his unique styles, how great food doesn't have to be rare nor incorporate expensive ingredients, and how fine cuisine should be defined not by mere price tags but by the chef's ability to transform ingredients with the far more priceless quality of imagination. It is in this spirit that many chefs have produced some of the most remarkably creative dishes, using never-before ingredients and pioneering cooking techniques.

Chef Atala also strives to break down mental barriers about food and uncover the character of the Amazonian wildlife in his dishes. Many of his creations carry deep meaning about his Brazilian roots. One of the most unforgettable dishes for me, is his famed *"golden Amazonian ants over a coconut meringue".* It actually looks just as phenomenal as it sounds. It was this dish that made me learn that cooking and eating ants was in fact a long-held native practice for indigenous groups in the Amazonian rainforests. Chef Atala's unfailing pursuit to present to the world such hidden gems and other of nature's fine offerings, is a constant source of inspiration for me and I believe many others. To me, there is no better way to respect the majestic Amazon than what he has done.

For every chef, what finally rounds up the experience of preparing a meal, is a wish that it feeds well and brings joy. Cooking demands attention and patience, and I think in its own right, qualifies as one of the most heartfelt and genuine acts of love. I recall with fond memories from my own experience working as a restaurant cook, the nervous glances at the faces of our diners whenever a dish you prepared was served to the tables. You get this rush of adrenaline and immense desire to witness the first mouthful bringing joy to your diners' faces.

"Good food is our common ground, a universal experience." Well said indeed by James Beard, American cook and champion of American cuisine. Eating is a basic human need, and enjoying food is one of the most inclusive experiences. Perhaps more than we tend to notice, food magically works its wonders, from comforting broken souls, uplifting downtrodden spirits to brightening the

darkest of times. It is no wonder that we celebrate most special occasions by feasting with our loved ones. And it is no surprise that some of the most renowned chefs still return to their mums' cooking for their favorite go-to meals. Food is so much more than just food. And I daresay it has gotten me smitten for life.

16

About Solitude

I come across as rather eccentric to most who know me, including closer friends and family. I have been commonly described as a person of extremes, seemingly operating in two modes and two modes only, one of piercing energy and extreme ecstasy, and the other being a state of uncomfortably deafening silence. You get the idea, I don't do in-betweens very well, it is either all or none. In this chapter, I'm inclined to talk more about the latter mode, i.e. the one of quiet solitude.

Solitude is to me, a blissfully meditative state. Instead of avoiding it like some others do, it falls snugly within my comfort zone. The state when I am most at ease is in my own lone presence. The kind of joy experienced in solitude is unique, and can be described as a kind of deep peaceful pleasure, as opposed to the relatively rambunctious euphoria that would otherwise often be the case in the presence of company.

There is something profoundly magical about a personal and quiet experience with nature and connecting with the 'aura' of your environment, or the 'feel' of the universe as I like to call it. This 'connection' remains a nebulous concept until you experience it for yourself. It is indeed something that is tricky to put down in words.

Psychologists have taken notice of an emerging profile of those who seek therapy. Unlike the typical stereotypes associated with having mental health issues, these patients are surprisingly well-heeled and polished individuals, often with respectable careers and stable demeanors. It is only upon further probing that underlying emotional ills are revealed, and they commonly point towards this feeling of 'emptiness'.

The feeling of emptiness is difficult to articulate, and hence succumbs easily to being brushed off. But the very prevalence of this mental burden, and increasing reports of more deleterious afflictions that eventually result (e.g. depression and addiction), all point towards the fact that it carries much greater weight than most of us imagine, and calls for more attention than is currently given.

The feeling of emptiness is not uncommon, but most people keep it hidden for obvious reasons, as it presents itself much as a 'weakness of character' that risks being exploited. The presence of an inner void feels like a barren emotional state, bereft of rolling passions, dry of ambition and purpose. It is a discomforting shroud of gloom, which may not feel acute enough to require attention, but weighs down heavily with each passing day, snowballing to breaking point when things turn awry.

Being out of touch with one's feelings is unnatural. Feelings are essential to life, and identifying with our emotions is a basic human condition. This modern malady of 'feeling empty' arises when we fail to acknowledge this natural need, and instead bury our emotions too deep, in hopes of being proudly looked upon as 'strong' or 'resilient'.

Unplug To Connect Inward

Societal demands weigh heavy on most of us, requiring our 24/7 attention and immediate response to calls for action. In the midst of fulfilling the desires of our cultural masters, we lose touch with our identities and cast aside our most fragile wants and needs.

Before any contemplation and 'inner work' can be done, it is necessary to unplug ourselves from external distractions. Most people struggle to take the first step of introspection as the fear of facing their inner world head on seems intractable. I can identify with that fear. As 17th century German poet, Johann Wolfgang von Goethe noted, *"nothing is more dangerous than solitude"*. As a matter of fact, extreme cases of isolation do at times result in deep despair, and even severe meltdowns. In fact, intentional mental torture operates on the basis of isolation, and is applied in punitive methods such as incarceration or exile. However these are extreme cases of isolation over long periods of time. As far as brief moments of quiet and relatively light-hearted solitude goes, we are more than safe.

Even if we do have to face up to our inner demons in our soul-searching, though uncomfortable at first, moderate amounts lead to many longer-term benefits. Being cognizant of our dark sides is the single most effective way to tame them and take full control over their effect on our thoughts and behaviors. Having this greater consciousness protects us from succumbing too easily to our own weaknesses and vices. It is often the level of self-awareness attained that determines the extent of understanding and compassion we can give to ourselves and others.

In Rainer Maria Rilke's "Letter to a Young Poet", he wrote about stepping up to the challenges that solitude may bring, *"you should not let yourself be confused in your solitude by the fact that there is some thing in you that wants to move out of it./ We must trust in what is difficult is a certainty that will never abandon us."*

Perception of Solitude

Even if one recognizes the benefits of solitude and is keen to practice it, there exists the barrier of societal perceptions, which alienates those who are seen in their own company. Solitude and separation are two different things, but few discern the difference. Society, both in the past till modern day, remains deeply entrenched in the way it operates in groups or 'cliques', and understandably so as we go about much of our lives in communities. However, we should be mindful that we remain masters of, and not slaves to the systems we create. In a mature society, every one of us should be free to exercise our right to uninterrupted and unjudged solitude, where the lonesome amongst us are not looked down upon, not labeled as strange, dangerous or unwanted.

Instead of looking upon those who prioritize solitude with disdain, we should instead acknowledge that they can in fact be one of the most mentally strong people around, and oftentimes, these people also have the most imaginative and creative minds. Solitude to the mind, is like bread and butter to the body. It is a time dedicated to being free from the demands of others, and when focus is returned back to an inner dialogue with ourselves.

In the quietness of solitude, one is safe from the watchful eye of another, free from the harshly critical and judgmental. It is in this safe space that one is better able to confront oneself in all honesty and with self-compassion and kindness. We are able to practice mindfulness and balanced awareness of our successes as well as sufferings, so that we may keep our egos in check for the former, and recognize and thereby release our pain for the latter. In Hamlet, one of Shakespeare's most influential works, he wrote, "to *thine own self be true, and it must follow, as the night the day, thou 'canst not then be false to any man."* Indeed, being true to others is predicated on first being true to oneself.

It is therefore during solitary moments that self-inquiry is deep, and through which our character is slowly and steadily forged, our virtues cultivated, and our life's purpose and meaning found. In the book "Solitude – A Return to Self", psychiatrist and author Anthony Storr explained how one finds meaning through what he creates during moments of solitude. He expressed that the most significant moments for the creative person in acquiring new insights are "*chiefly, if not invariably, those in which he is alone."*

Indeed many wise and hugely accomplished men before us have personally attested to the value of leaving time to being with just ourselves alone and retiring to the peace and quiet in the privacy of our own presence. For Albert

Einstein, one of the greatest physicist the world has ever seen, it was during these moments that he claimed to draw his imagination from, and in his own words, *"If my work isn't going well, I lie down in the middle of the workday and gaze at the ceiling while I listen and visualize what is going on inside my imagination."* Nikola Tesla, another exceptional intellectual with tremendous contributions in the area of science and engineering, similarly proclaimed, *"No big laboratory is needed in which to think./ Be alone, that is the secret of invention; be alone, that is when ideas are born."*

Final Thoughts

In ending, I would like to leave you with a brief extract from the poem *"On Drinking Wine"* by Eastern Jin dynasty poet Tao Yuan Ming, as I think it conveys so simply yet profoundly, the richness gained from plain, unadorned solitude. As he reminisced about plucking chrysanthemums from the eastern hedge and gazing into the southern mountain, he expressed, *"In such things we find true meaning, but when I try to explain, I can't find the words."*

17

About Friendships

Friendship - one of the most common relationships between people, so common that wanting to discuss more about it may raise an eyebrow. Yet, what a curious little thing. I call it a thing, for it is actually incredibly difficult to define.

Aristotle, one of most influential philosophers of all time, termed friendship as a virtue that was essential to life, *"for without friends no one would choose to live though he had all other goods"*. He opined that bearing goodwill to each other constitutes the bedrock of friendship. More specifically, he expressed that friendships based on virtue lay superior to those based on advantage or pleasure alone, for friendships are marked by companionship, dependability and trust above mutual benefit. For Plato, another godfather of ancient Greek philosophy, friendship goes further as to escape definition, due to its nature as more a process rather than an object. That is, a process that seeks to know the other.

In fact, the line between friendship and the next most known type of relationship, marriage, starts to blur when we view them through the lenses of love in all its forms. What first comes to mind to most of us when we speak of love I assume is sexual love, or *eros*. That intoxicating and amorous love we experience in a romantic relationship. We then have *storge*, or familial love, which arises from the natural bonds between familiar members of family. As for the love between friends in the case of friendship, it is also known as *philia*, and is often argued as one of the higher-level loves due to its freely chosen nature and relative lack of a specific purpose or mutual gain. And finally, for the sake of completeness, the final and less-common love form to mention here would be *agape* or universal love - a respectable and noble form of love that transcends boundaries and extends unconditionally to all of nature; family, friends, and even total strangers and animals. It is essentially a selfless love, not predicated on blood ties, cultural affiliations, familiarity or mutual benefit.

As one of the most practiced love forms, friendship is ironically one of the least natural of loves. *Philia*, usually borne out of shared interests and values, is based almost entirely on personal selection. As C.S. Lewis described, it is "*the least instinctive, organic, biological, gregarious and necessary. We can breed without friendship and carry on existence without it.*" So wherein lies the distinction between friendship and romantic relationships, and will our lives be held in any less regard, be any less enriched if fulfilled by friendships alone, sans *eros*? Or should the question perhaps be, does *philia* rank inferior, and should it?

C.S Lewis went further to point out that "*friendship is unnecessary, like philosophy, like art.... It has no survival value; rather it is one of those things which give value to survival.*" Instead of playing second fiddle and quite on the contrary, *philia* in its pure form, outshines most other loves. Devoid of undercurrents of selfish desire, jealous possession, or motives and intention, the quality of *philia* is supreme and almost unmatched. It is no wonder that the concept of friendship was featured centrally in Plato's most famous dialogue, "The Republic", written around 380BC. In there, he emphasized the enriching nature that an abundance of friendship connections has on society as a whole, and tears down notions of a city-family conflict. *"The whole city simply is the family"*. According to Plato, citizens should hold a widespread devotion towards all others and spread love based on their civic virtue rather than on their personal selves. Surpassing specific family attachment, the love between citizens should carry only each other's genuine interests at heart. He further surmised that in an ideal society, the success of others would be perceived as contributory towards one's own success.

A widely adored and somewhat romanticized aspect of erotic love, is an expectation of eternity. This is apparent not only in the sanctity of marriage vows which are focused on a long-term commitment of undying union, but also features strongly in society's general acknowledgement that real love should embody absolute alignment and last a lifetime. How many of us have encountered before, resentment and disorientation in our relationships due to a failure to live up to suffocating ideals which we hold so religiously to? It is with understanding that we find ourselves sometimes retreating into the comfort and ease of relatively fuss-free friendships instead.

Just because a relationship is unable to last forever does not diminish the quality of what was once had. As with most things in life, nothing is permanent. It is in fact more natural to expect a beginning and an end. Much like the ephemeral moments of blooming cherry blossoms, some of life's most beautiful moments are extremely short-lived, yet no less beautiful. Succumbing to the pressure of marriage for the sole sake of claiming a false sense of eternal bondage would simply be an act of setting ourselves up for upset.

The above said, I do not however deny the numerous virtues of marriage and the benefits of long-term relationships. But this need not preclude accepting the possibility of having genuine and loving relationships despite them being non-romantic and relatively short-lived. As famed filmmaker Jean-Luc Godard astutely observed, *"a story should have a beginning, a middle and an end, but not necessarily in that order."* Recognizing the realities of love and being open in loving would provide that much more breathing space for us to love more freely and be genuinely fulfilled from the love we give and receive.

Perhaps, before we get too melancholic about the seriousness of it all, we should take a step back and revisit the seemingly tongue-in-cheek yet startlingly insightful quote by Danish philosopher Kierkegaard, *"marry, and you will regret it; don't marry, you will also regret it; marry or don't marry, you will regret it either way."* For most things in life, whatever the choice we eventually make, it is going to be painful for pain is simply part and parcel of living. The choice for us isn't so much between happiness and suffering, but between the types of suffering we would ultimately prefer.

As final food for thought, I figured it would be worthwhile sharing German philosopher Erich Fromm's refreshing take on the realities of (romantic) love - *"There is hardly any activity, any enterprise, which is started with such tremendous hopes and expectations, and yet, which fails so regularly, as love."*

18

About Special Occasions

One of the clear signs of entering into your early thirties, for me at least, is that steadily increasing presence at friend's weddings and baby shower parties. It is always heartwarming to witness the joy of your beloved family and friends, and I enjoy immersing in the infective cheer and high spirits so well captured at such celebrations. Not to mention the extra benefit of gathering together with long-neglected friends for a light-hearted catch-up and fond rehash of old times. Indeed, celebrations have long played its part well in bringing together communities while honoring significant life events. Celebrations in general provide precious opportunities for us to commemorate pivotal life events, in the presence of preferred company.

One especially popular conversation topic at a recently-attended wedding left me with particular impression. It was the topic of celebrations and ceremonies. The conversations went down a path of light-hearted jibes and self-deprecating grouses, with a general sentiment of resignation to the increasingly-felt strains of modern rituals which have seemingly evolved from their more organic intents and headed for the worse.

In Mitch Albom's wildly popular memoir, "Tuesdays with Morrie", he chronicles the time spent with his aged professor Morrie Schwartz who was dying from Amyotrophic Lateral Sclerosis, a progressive neurodegenerative disease. In his book, he noted his teacher's wise words about how the culture we have today diminishes basic self-worth, and pushes us into placing value on the wrong things, leading us to very disillusioned lives. This phenomenon has in fact become so pervasive that one has to actively resist its influence, and be *strong enough to say if the culture doesn't work, don't buy it.* The extremes to which some prevailing customs and practices have spiraled into, really beg question if status quos have degenerated into pursuits of mindless habit carrying little identifiable meaning.

While I'm definitely not against honoring special events and indulging in occasional celebrations, remaining mindful about the 'why's and 'how's of celebrations can be easily missed amidst the hype of festivities. Mindfulness in fact, might just be the one true way of giving due justice to the sacredness of the very occasions being celebrated. Judging from how things have evolved, it doesn't take much to see that something is clearly amiss when the fulfillment of customary niceties has to come at tremendous personal expense. This phenomenon is not only apparent in the happier occasions of weddings and birthdays, but also extend into more somber events such as funerals.

Sentimentality can be dangerous, especially when mixed with spending decisions. It is not difficult to understand the temptations of emotional spending especially when it involves matters of the heart. For lack of better outlets to release pent-up emotions, be it from the grief of a lost love or the joy of a lifelong union like marriage, we can easily allow our better judgments to be obscured and succumb to irrational degrees of mindless spending. Many of us have no problems kidding ourselves into believing that the dollars given up prescribe meaning and worth to these significant events, and we therefore easily latch on to the emotional closure that sentimental purchases offer.

I am unfortunately myself a victim of irrational purchases. I wouldn't say I am alone in this, for it occurs as a somewhat imprinted cultural condition that few can dissociate with. We are all too familiar with the nagging guilt when thoughts of cost-saving creep up, especially for items like engagement rings and birthday cakes. More morbidly, when faced with the death of a loved one, spending offers solace that helps fill that inner void. As for happier events like birthdays, displays of exorbitance and big-bang styles shore up the self-fulfilling assurance that we have given rightful respect to the special people or events in our lives. Herein however lies a slight problem, the focus of our energies has become *how* we spend the occasion, instead of the occasion itself.

When we over-glamorize special occasions, we may at the same time subconsciously dampen the significance of every other day. What we choose to celebrate is in fact a man-made construct. There are certainly no limits to the creativity of ideas on this front, from the widely recognized Valentine's Days to more bizarre celebrations like the La Pourcailhade (Festival of the Pig) in France and La Tomatina (Tomato Throwing Festival) in Spain. Sometimes, there is actually very little consideration behind cause for celebration. It may well be perfectly fine for us to meddle less and simply allow the significance of special occasions to speak for themselves.

Let's take for example the much-celebrated New Year's Eve. Most would agree on its wholesome intent to mark new beginnings and renew resolutions for a successful new year. However, when celebrations are taken to the extreme, we sometimes get lost in the fanfare. Recall that familiar ritual of staying up late into the night, drinking ourselves silly, and over-indulging on party snacks. Our hopes for a better tomorrow ironically runs counter to the mortifying mess we get ourselves into just the day before. While I'm not advocating being strait-laced and prudish about it, I think we could afford to pull back a little when our party poppers dim the greater significance of the event itself.

Another occasion famously known to be a nightmare of a financial burden is none other than the formidable wedding. The hugely inflated 'new normal's of wedding standards have sadly become suffocating to say the least. From ostentatious rings, globetrotting wedding photography tours to lavish banquets, it is no surprise that one can chalk up a huge sum (or should I say debt) all for that single day. So ingrained are these practices that slight suggestions to opt out of any of these "standard elements" are quite keenly perceived as travesty, and unfortunately most often by the very people we want to impress. Don't get me wrong for I have no intention to scorn the sanctity of marriage nor advocate jettisoning the ceremony altogether. Quite on the contrary, I believe in commemorating this sacred union and once-in-a-lifetime celebration of love. That said, I do find it disturbing hearing stories of friends suffering immensely behind the glitz and glamour of their weddings. It occurs as paradoxically tragic to me that the supposed happiest day of a couple's life together should commence with such stress and burden. The essence of celebrating a couple's love and in marking a new beginning has become blurred by an obsession for perfection in every detail in hopes to impress. I think it is worth rethinking our tendencies before we drive ourselves into greater delusions that run counter to the true meaning of the occasion.

Other than weddings, I have some notoriously unpopular views on the touchy topic of funerals. The widely adored Anne Frank expressed my exact sentiments in her famous diary, "The Diary of Anne Frank", where she honestly put *"Dead people receive more flowers than the living ones because the regret is stronger than gratitude."*

Pardon me for going into some depth on the topic of death here, but I don't think there is anything really unsettling nor fearful about death. It is simply natural and necessary, even liberating for those suffering and battling illness. Funeral practices, to me, are largely self-fulfilling. Tending to our living moments occurs to me as far more meaningful than any amount of spending or elaborate arrangement after death. It is just that the living who are left behind find no better closure than seeing the amount of money and effort spent on funerals as a measure of their love for the deceased. The more that one spends on expensive coffins, funeral processions and the like, the more dignity is perceived to have been accorded to the dead. But however I think about it, I find these actions only self-serving for the living, and admittedly they have proved effective in filling that emotional void and sense of loss. These actions however, neither benefit nor have any effect on the dead.

While there is no doubt that we ought to pay due respect to the dead, that does not preclude questioning if material outpourings appropriately express this intent. By virtue of the fact that dignity and respect originate from the heart, they could simply and sufficiently be expressed just as well, if not perhaps even more genuinely, in a silent and heartfelt prayer.

19

About Education

"I have never let my schooling interfere with my education," said one of the most celebrated writers in history, Mark Twain.

Education - a topic that rarely fails as a conversation starter. Education is personal, gets personal, and so deeply resonates with most people. Perhaps because we all subconsciously vest great hopes in posterity, this topic carries extraordinary weight in our hearts.

Education is one of the only means familiar to us, which we can within our control and in our lifetimes, attempt our best effort at in preparing our young ones for the big unknowns of the future. Whether we have been going about it effectively, or are instead unknowingly traversing a grossly misguided path, we will never know at least until much later. That said, even if we have not gotten it completely right straightaway, we should at all times, try to be less wrong about it than we could.

One of the most beautiful things about children is in their pureness. It is no wonder that it is also one of the scariest tasks to raise them well when entrusted with such vulnerability. Their fearless openness to knowledge, voracious appetite for learning, and delicate mouldability, naturally weigh heavy on their forebears' attempts to educate them well. French-Canadian writer, Gabrielle Roy wrote about the vulnerability of children and how it was *"on their frail shoulders that we loaded the weight of our weary hopes and eternal new beginnings"*. Like fragile flowers, children deserve nothing less than careful nurturing and protection from the overwhelming deluge of modern-day ills, yet all this without casting a shadow over the realities of life.

We can all relate to that familiar saying *"It is easier to build strong children than to repair broken men."* With education possessing such power, with the potential to leave the most significant and lasting imprints on a person's life, one can understand why this topic draws much attention and opinion.

I do not claim to have been educated extremely well myself, although for most people, mine would probably pass off as decent enough. Nonetheless, it is still constantly a question on my mind – the question about what good education really means. While I have been through quite extensive formal education and conventional schooling, I only have very vague "hunches" about what an ideal education entails.

My early years of schooling come close to what I would quite unforgivingly but honestly describe as run-of-the-mill affair - uninteresting and plain vanilla. It was an uneventful sequence of events, as I trudged along the path laid out for me, like clockwork going from kindergarten to primary and secondary schools, then to tertiary education. Even in writing, I couldn't make it sound any more exciting. While I did fine in school, unbeknownst to many was that I did not enjoy the experience of formal schooling. I hung on only because I had been too cowardly to contemplate veering into any alternative paths less traveled. It was therefore unsurprising that I found myself sucked into a system that eventually took from me in exchange, my blazing spirit. Fortunately, this turned out to be only temporary for my perennially raging inner fire proved to be way more stubborn than I imagined.

As much as I deplore systems of control, being in one (whether voluntarily or not) meant I had to abide by the rules, as a matter of principle. I consider myself lucky to have survived the long-drawn rite of passage within the confines of schooling systems, an experience I would describe, although quite possibly to the chagrin of many stalwarts of conventional schooling, a "dumbing-down process" for the most part. Fortunately, I came out of all that sufficiently unscathed, or so I think, with my pocketful of rebellious ways ending up becoming quite a lifebuoy throughout.

As with every traumatic experience, the aftermath often leaves you in some kind of solemn contemplation. It occurred to me one day as I spoke to some friends about school days (those I would rather forget), that there was this common thread of human behavior that would always end up as one of the major culprits for ruining well-meaning plans and intentions. Humans just can't resist complicating matters for no good reason. And I'm in no way suggesting that I am separate from this propensity either, but am simply verbalizing a personal observation of a recurrent human habit. Simple and intuitive ways to go about living a peacefully enriched life, when passed through human hands, can somehow turn into something pretty awry. Take for example education since we are on this topic. Something as natural as learning about the world can be controlled to the point of, ironically, a complete loss of control. The innate human desire to discover about the world around us can be so tragically crushed at the hands of none other than ourselves and our self-righteous systems. To top it all off, we convince ourselves with a truckload of self-comforting and romanticized falsehoods.

In the area of education, we are not unfamiliar with the overplayed narrative about developing critical thinking, fostering curiosity, building character …and the list goes on. I find the biggest irony in that I actually only experienced the true joy of learning after I was finally free from the clutches of formal education. Reclaiming control over my energy, time and imagination to explore and learn about anything I wanted to on my own terms, felt natural and produced unparalleled results. It actually was as simple as having the freedom to maneuver.

Silly Authority and Rules

I used to be pretty arrogant as a kid, some probably think I still am. Senseless instruction and mindless authority just never sat well with me. In my defense, it wasn't that much of an ignorant defiance but more a conscious refusal to accede to nonsense masquerading as 'required conduct'. I recall pet phrases in the likes of 'because I told you so' and 'everyone does that' which were much adored by teachers and disciplinarians. The use of authority to gain a free pass on exerting influence, whether considered or not, wasn't something I easily indulged. Strangely however, I was often alone in these sentiments. Many of my peers were coping much better following what they were told. While this did offer superficial comfort, it carried more insidious undertones. The very attitude of resignation, especially if ingrained at a young age, eventually snowballs into a much more intractable problem later in life. When default apathy and mechanical obedience become the order of the day, we have a real problem on our hands. The subconscious reliance on the approval of others becomes an emotional crutch, and we forget the value of disagreement for personal growth. It is often those who do not approve of us, who will help us discover and define ourselves. And it is both inescapable and necessary to learn to manage difference and discord, for they are part and parcel of life.

For me, I had been lucky in the sense that I got by with decent grades, so most of my teachers left me alone. But I remain empathetic towards those who suffer poorer fates. The most obedient ones usually suffer the most from the suffocation of an iron fist rule, and understandably so. Joseph Agassi, an Israeli academic shed some related insight in his book "The Hazard Called Education". He wrote *"when a teacher sends a child to the headmaster, everybody knows as a matter of course that the child is in the wrong."* In this example, he alluded to how, as commonplace the said occurrence was, it ran contrary to the expectations of a civilized society and dare I say, even to basic common sense. Agassi went further to identify schools as *"total institutions of sorts"*, where his point was that school children were akin to inmates at the mercy of compulsory education laws. I wouldn't say there are no truths in his words.

The above said, I do not mean to imply that mandatory schooling should be scraped. On the contrary, I believe schooling is both necessary and critical in preparing our youth to continue good work in progressing mankind. However, I do think that schools could and should do better where it concerns tuning in to the needs of those being schooled. We must not forget that the vulnerable young minds at the receiving end of formal teaching, are having extremely important decisions made for them, with repercussions only exclusively affecting them. The very children receiving what schooling prescribes, are rarely participant to the process of designing the systems for learning.

Towards those younger than ourselves, we adults do generally possess an air of vehemence in our insistence of what should be right and wrong. We are often guilty of dispensing quite liberally with absolute judgments, in the name of teaching or mentoring a younger one. Irish philosopher, Edmund Burke once said, *"the arrogance of age must submit to be taught by youth."* Children are young, no doubt, and many use that as convenient excuse to equate a lack of self-governing competence. However, authorities and teachers calling the shots are in fact none the wiser. Children are simply very young human beings. The mere fact that they are human beings just like any one of us, justifies claim to their rightful moral status, and for that matter, there are things that should not be done to them for the plain reason that their human rights should be respected no less. I find it odd that obvious violations of this basic right are allowed to run rampant, and even perpetuate through generations in such open and widely-accepted fashion in education.

Virtue Education

"Educating the mind without educating the heart is no education at all" says Aristotle. If there was one thing that schools should focus on especially early on in a young adult's life, it should be to cultivate virtues, over and above downloading knowledge. Michel de Montaigne, one of the most endearing philosophers of the French Renaissance, underscored the importance of this in simple terms, that *"every other knowledge is harmful to him who does not have knowledge of goodness."*

Unlike knowledge, which is as fleeting as yesterday's news, values stay with a child for life. They serve as their beacon of light guiding their every decision, and their moral compass protecting their faith and integrity against the onslaught of modern-day distractions, misinformed messages, and luring temptations of egoism, greed and hatred. I think what the world needs aren't more walking dictionaries, 'enlightened hedonists' nor 'high-performing spiritual infants'. What humanity is really starved of, is much more basic and much less complicated. We just need more respect, compassion and tolerance to go around, for that is how we flourish as a community.

Character building isn't about attending a seven-day crash course filled with back-to-back lectures and silly thirty-minute games. True character development is an enduring process, starting early in a young child when values are imparted, and these values are allowed time to grow, deepen and embed in the child's psyche as he progresses into adulthood. The saving grace is that many of these values can be learnt, and it is precisely befitting that academic institutions should see virtue education as one of their top priorities. I quote Bill Bullard, former Dean of Faculty for the San Francisco University High School, where he expressed that *"the highest form of knowledge... is empathy, for it requires us to suspend our egos and live in another's world."* He wanted to convey the essence of empathy and its profound purpose, which was far greater than the self-absorbed kind of understanding. As parents busy themselves with packing their kids' schedules with all kinds of extra-curricular activities and so-called enrichment classes, do they recall the last time there was a specific agenda set for simply practicing being a good person?

Curiosity & Creativity

I find it puzzling that most schools manage to operate chiefly at two extremes, and never really succeeding in achieving that magic in the middle. For the student, you often either turned to disinterest after a prolonged rule under archaic instruction, or suffered a self-eroding sense of defeatedness as you succumbed to being patronized in your every action and thought. It is ironic how schools have managed to produce outcomes so far off from their proudly proclaimed objectives. It is similarly confounding that our deeply cogitated education systems and highly regarded institutions of learning, could veer so far off-track, especially when backed by an army of supposed intellectuals and highly-qualified educational practitioners.

Most of us acknowledge that every child is born with extraordinary talent. Like splashes of color, each person brings to humanity his unique shade. It is therefore ever more crushing when one has to witness this magnificence get buried into oblivion.

One of the key elements to self-motivated lifelong learning is intrinsic curiosity. Without which, our schools would be nothing but temporary crutches which only leave one later handicapped, not out of circumstance, poor fate or bad luck, but more self-imposed, a consequence of misguided conditioning.

It is a tragedy when young children harbor an excessive fear of being 'wrong'. What makes it harder to bear is witnessing their resignation to the illusion of failure, and the obliteration of any remaining shred of wonderment and awe they initially had.

Any false representations of what is deemed 'correct' or the 'truth' are potentially dangerous, as they unnecessarily tear down the self-assuredness we need to explore the unknown and expand our boundaries. Alluding to one of 20th century philosopher Sir Karl Raimund Popper's most reputed theories, any solution offered for a problem cannot be demonstrated to be the absolute truth, and no amount of evidence could justify, verify, nor confirm the truth of any given theory. Even for what we may think are eternal truths, there was no way for us, as imperfect human beings, to deny the possibility that at some future time, what is known to be the 'truth' will be improved or superseded by some unknown or yet to be created or discovered idea.

Hence in a way, there is no 'truth' to speak of in learning, and what is taught in schools should avoid being framed as the last word in human understanding. To me, the bottomline is that education should spur curiosity and creativity. The worst that could happen would be to not only fail in this endeavor, but also wind up 'educating' people out of their remaining creative capacities.

The Trap of Intellect

In most developed cultures, the highly prized intellectual mind is worshipped and idolized. Most of society reverently place education and the educated high on the pedestal. We are most familiar with this when it comes to job-hunting, for example. The pride of laying claim to a degree from an Ivy League school, and the adulation received from a glorious display of perfect scores are what drive many to seek such honours.

The growing appeal of degrees and qualifications has driven the phenomenon of 'academic inflation'. Academic pedigrees have now become widely confused with intelligence, and those who boast glamorous credentials are looked upon as esteemed saviors of societal problems. From governments to general population to our own parents, we are collectively obsessed with hustling people up the ladder of academia.

Don't get me wrong for I do not deny the value of an academic experience. In fact, I have personally only stood to gain tremendously from it myself. What I am however cautioning against is an overzealous obsession that obscures our original intentions for seeking academic honors in the first place. I am wary about whether, amidst the rat race, we are still mindful of our larger purposes and goals in life. As Martin Luther King Jr said, *"Nothing in the world is more dangerous than sincere ignorance and conscientious stupidity."* A robotic march towards the top of the education pyramid with no clear aim, would only leave us caught in the 'trap of intellect'.

In fact long before our time, early sages had begun contemplating the concept of intellectual ambition. One of them was Saint Thomas Aquinas, a 12th century Italian theologian and philosopher who sought to return emphasis to personal observation and experience in learning. He identified the common trap of "intellectual snobbery" where we dismiss a piece of information or given idea due to our own judgments of its source. Aquinas sought to remind us to guard against the folly of equating the imagery in our minds as reality, citing the analogy that a person *"who accepts the Church as an infallible guide will believe whatever the Church teaches."* Even today, some of us are guilty of dismissing information based on preconceived notions about their source. This would be a crime equivalent to disregarding someone based on outward appearance, place of origin, or any other characteristics irrelevant to the subject matter being assessed.

Michel de Montaigne brought further awakening to the concept of freely entertaining doubt, and also in the most candid of ways. He sought to caution us against getting too much ahead of ourselves such that we get lost in our own pedantry and arrogance. He espoused simplicity and being in touch with reality over an elitist scholarly culture, and reminded us that *"on the highest throne in the world, we are seated, still, upon our arses."* Like his gems of wisdom, his unique way with words is never short of allure.

Montaigne sought to impress upon us the individual intelligence we all innately possess, and that true worth of anything is measured by its usefulness and appropriateness to life, sans veneers. Wisdom is no more elusive than we are made to imagine and like what Alain De Botton, Swiss-born British author well-regarded for his discussions on contemporary subjects and modern day philosophy, said, *"a virtuous, ordinary life, striving for wisdom but never far from folly, is achievement enough."*

Crammed Timetables

I think most schooling systems are currently impoverished by design. Let's start with ill-planned timetables. Studies have shown that the typical human brain can hold no more than seven pieces of new information for less than 30 seconds. I am sure most of us have heard about the famed 'learning curve', which describes the relationship between memory and time. In essence, it postulates that if one's absorption rate were 100 percent on day one, then there would be a 50 to 80 percent loss of learning from the second day onward. This is then further reduced to a retention rate of only 2 to 3 percent at the end of thirty days. Armed with such insight, perhaps it is with good reason we should revisit how school timetables are planned.

Rote Memorization

The lackluster results of rote memorization in achieving learning objectives have become more widely recognized of late. It is not difficult to understand why. In reality, the world does not operate in a vacuum of information. In fact, we suffer quite the opposite, i.e. an information explosion. As such, the conditions under which rote memorization would be necessary in real life would probably almost never come about. Yet, in practice, we still find difficulty in shedding old ways that no longer serve us.

John Medina, author of "Brain Rules", brought our attention to the fact that in the previous few decades, our sloppiness on rote learning has become apparent. He articulated the crux of the memorization problem when he expressed it as necessary only if there was something to improvise off of, *"otherwise you are simply playing air guitar."* To me, rote memorization not only squanders precious time that could be better spent going about actual learning, but even worse, it crushes any zest for learning. *"Those who have been required to memorize the world as it is will never create the world as it might be,"* said Judith Groch, author of "The Right to Create".

I recall my own experience of spending many precious hours of my youth force-feeding my brain with inconsequential facts that had to be cast into memory. It was such a painful process that I do not wish unto anyone, especially for no good reason.

Hopes for the Future

"If you wanted to create an education environment that was directly opposed to what the brain was good at doing, you probably would design something like a classroom," said John Medina, author of "Brain Rules". Children should not need to be sat down and taught. They, more than any of us, are spontaneous observers of nature, and learning about the world is their second nature. Learning is an organic process and should rightfully remain so. Given the right conditions, it happens naturally and without effort. To quote none other than the great Albert Einstein, who claimed to never teach his students, *"[I] only attempt to provide the conditions in which they can learn."*

Final Thoughts

It is unfortunate that less savory memories of my school days have stayed with me. On the bright side, these recollections have helped me empathize better with those caught in similar predicaments. I have made a personal pact that if and when the right opportunity to effect positive change comes about on matters pertaining to education, I would strive to do my utmost. For my biggest regret would be that innocent generations after us endure the same idiocy that we have been put through.

20

About Death

My apologies for putting a much-avoided word in the title for this chapter. I couldn't find a better word. Yes, this chapter is about death. It has always been my wish to spend a good few moments acknowledging death, and hopefully through my feeble attempt with whatever words I can muster, I would give it its due respect.

The very result of recognizing the significance of death brings out the beauty of life. I like to ponder my own final moments for it gives me much strength during my weakest times. The concept of death is worth discussing, for it helps frame our minds to pursue love, meaning and richness in our fleeting journey through life.

I used to be a hopeless perfectionist. While I still carry strands of it, I would say I've become much more relaxed. It isn't straightforward to master the art of letting go. Some may go as far as to regard it as one of the higher-level spiritual goals in life. To be adept at accepting and letting go, amidst constant striving, is by far one of the most challenging balancing acts of the mind. I think Chinese philosopher Lao Tzu wrote about this extremely well in one of the verses of the Tao Te Ching, where he expressed that everything under Heaven is a sacred vessel and cannot be controlled. In essence, he wanted us to notice that there was a time for everything, from the good to the bad, that there was a time for being ahead and a time for being behind. *"In trying to grasp, we lose, allow life to unfold naturally"*.

This verse is powerful in conveying profound messages with great clarity. I have personally dictated it to myself so many times that it would be embarrassing to reveal the count. Life, put simply, should exist ideally as a cycle between two states – passionate pursuit and nonchalant acceptance. The former propels us into the future with spirited optimism, while the latter allows us to be at peace with the past.

Many of our problems are completely imagined and self-created. We are often consumed by personal greed and the compulsion to take excessive control of what is in fact much beyond our grasp. This happens especially when we lose faith in the greater wisdom acting beyond us. Selfish desires manifest themselves in various forms and quickly spiral into a vicious cycle of superficial material dependence that ultimately leads only to agony. It has happened enough times in my own experience for me to believe that the less I pursue something, the more I enjoy of its abundance. It sounds like a feel-good self-deceiving mantra, but I can only say that it has miraculously and irrationally proven to be the case. When you turn over control to the universe and simply allow life to happen, troubles naturally dissolve. As the saying goes, *"If it comes, let it. If it goes, let it"*. Although admittedly, this requires a strong will and intentional 'unplugging' from the strong influences of cultural conditioning and commercial messaging which surround us.

Contemplating death as a meditative thought is a savior more than taboo. Our worldly desires almost instantly and quite unceremoniously reduce to nothing, when juxtaposed with death. Such is the incredible soft power of absolute finality. Few of us may have noticed but since time immemorial, artists have produced works that served to remind us about death. Also referred to as *"memento mori"*, the aim of such works wasn't to depress people about their eventual demise, as if life hadn't thrown enough at them already. The beauty of this art lay in its ability to provide access to experiences that would otherwise be difficult to get hold of. They gently remind us about the equalizing and uncompromising endpoint to our time here, and in so doing, place the spotlight back on purposeful living as life is pared down to its core.

To quote Morrie in Mitch Albom's book "Tuesdays with Morrie" as he shares his final moments, *"Don't cling to things because everything is impermanent... But detachment doesn't mean you don't let the experience penetrate you."* He went further to explain that it was in feeling deeply and experiencing thoroughly, that we are able to truly let go. It is indeed the ones who face imminent death who offer the most priceless and unembellished insights.

Transience of Life

One of the cardinal truths we so conveniently forget is the transient nature of life. Most of us would rationally not wish that tragedy befall us just to comprehend this piece of wisdom. Thankfully, our imagination in this case would suffice in refocusing our attention back on our rightful priorities and triggering greater awareness of the many miracles that already surround us.

Appreciation is always easier said than done. Amidst the chaos and stresses of modern life, most of us struggle just to retain some quiet time in solitude to straighten our thoughts. It really isn't that life is too short, as we like to tell ourselves. As Roman philosopher Seneca pointed out, *"Life, if well lived, is long enough"*. A man with gray hairs and wrinkles has in fact just existed long, but not necessarily lived long. No matter how long we exist, it will never be enough if we are unclear about what we intend to achieve nor how to go about it. Consider how much time we squander in fruitless activities and how much energy we dedicate to amassing inconsequential material goods. There is much that we hold on to compulsively, which we do not truly desire but are instead coerced into thinking are necessary. It is no wonder that to many of us, life is too short. For we made it so.

Experience over Possession

"The whole future lies in uncertainty: live immediately," said Roman philosopher, Seneca. It is frequently the case that people pursue possessions, instead of capture the less tangible value of experience. Depending on your focus, it can lead to vastly different lives. Regardless of our age, we bear the personal responsibility to design our lives with intention, and this endeavor should take immediate effect. We often deprive ourselves of the basic freedom to act, as we trap ourselves in the illusion that only after attaining

certain milestones through meaningless pursuits, are we entitled to organize our lives in the way we desire.

"I freed a thousand slaves. I could have freed a thousand more if only they knew they were slaves," said Harriet Tubman, American bondwoman who escaped slavery in the South to become a leading abolitionist before the American Civil War. I think we are living in an age of widespread slavery in a much more insidious form - mental slavery. When I was in my previous desk-bound job working the typical 9 to 5, I felt a deep sense of self-neglect. It was in the way that you felt your time, which is also your life's most prized currency, was forcibly seized and thoughtlessly squandered. Even though many may frown upon the fact that I left my well-paying job at its perceived peak, only the wise amongst them will discern who stood to gain the most out of it.

A Life Well-Lived

Contemplating death paradoxically forces us to learn to live better. The difficulty however doesn't lie in the contemplation itself, but in getting our heads around our self-defeating excuses and self-imposed restrictions. Most of us listen only to what we want to hear, and believe as much as what we already set out to believe. No amount of extrinsic force is greater than an innate intention.

Acknowledging our innate intelligence and having faith in our potential are key to accessing the true value of our existence. *"No amount of security is worth the suffering of a mediocre life chained to a routine that has killed your dreams,"* said Maya Mendoza, author of "The Hidden Power of Emotional Intuition". In all of the chaos that surrounds us, we must resist losing sight of the one true north that lies within all of us, the unfailing inner compass that spells our identity and holds the essence of our existence.

When we begin to align ourselves with goals much larger than our mortality, and much more eternal than our own lifespans, we put our existence back in perspective as part of the larger universe. Like how Eckart Tolle, German-born author of "The Power of Now and A New Earth" said, *"You are the universe, expressing itself as a human for a little while".* For don't we all originate from the same beginning, i.e. birth, and face the common fate, i.e. death. So how different are we really? We are all but part of a human family, and it will never be wrong to invest our living moments in people and relationships rather than in material pursuits. *"You live on - in the hearts of everyone you have touched and nurtured while you were here... Death ends life, not a relationship,"* expressed Mitch Albom in "Tuesdays with Morrie". Never sell yourself short for your life is worthy of nothing less than everything you've got with every living breath.

The Taboo About Death

"The oldest and strongest kind of fear is fear of the unknown." - American author, H.P. Lovecraft

Thoughts about death should not scare us. For me, I learnt to embrace death much more warmly after reading about Near-Death Experiences (NDEs). You would be surprised at the extraordinary stories that have been retold by those who survived close brushes with death to tell the tale. And interestingly enough, these people have been reported to have lost the fear of death, and gained a renewed perception towards life and consciousness. If what they experienced was anywhere near as traumatic as what most of us imagine it to be, I'm sure their refreshing perspectives would not have been intuitive.

Personally, one of the key takeaways from learning about others' NDEs was to always refrain from judging what I do not know enough of, and to be open enough to even question my own perceived rational mind. I do not think that most of those who survived to recount their NDEs have a good reason to lie. It is up to us to learn as much as we are willing to.

Greek philosopher, Epicurus argued against the fear of death, *"Death does not concern us, because as long as we exist, death is not here. And when it does come, we no longer exist."* Assuming one's life ends at death, then there should be nothing to fear since we no longer exist to experience pain or pleasure in the first place. Perhaps, it is more about the pain and suffering that precedes death that we are afraid of, rather than death itself. Or to be even more precise, it is the much-dreaded regret from failure to tie up loose ends before our permanent departure that creates a taboo out of the notion of death. To paraphrase German poet Bertolt Brecht, we do not fear death so much, but rather the inadequate life.

21

About Appearance

"Do not judge by appearances but judge with right judgment." - John 7:24

We live in a very blessed time, and I mean it in terms of being in this technology age. Typing on our computers, tapping on our smartphones and sending emails on the go, are all second nature to most of us. The sophisticated software, state-of-the-art gadgets and lightning-speed connectivity are to us what bricks and stones were to the ancient Egyptians. This modern day modus operandi would have drawn wide-eyed awe just decades ago.

A popular catch phrase sometimes used to describe this phenomenon is that 'the world is flattening'. It is now possible for people from all around the world, including complete strangers living oceans apart, to communicate and collaborate in real time. Technology, the great equalizer, has created a level playing field at an unprecedented global scale, shrinking the world from a size large to a size zero within a fraction of our evolution timescale.

Before I go too deep belaboring the awesomeness of the cyber age, let me bring myself back on track to drawing attention specifically to how technology has done wonders in connecting us with ease to people from all over, especially those whom we previously would never have imagined to be acquainted with in our wildest dreams. Amidst all the bad rap that technology has received in terms of its repercussions on society and its moral fiber, I intend to instead focus on some particular merits that technology has brought, and more specifically, how it has helped dilute our cognitive biases based on external attributes.

So what is this cognitive bias? I'm alluding to the 'halo effect', which describes the overall impression that one has on another person based on outward appearance or other external qualities, which are then used to judge the person's character. This remains one of the most influential stereotypes operating in our subconscious. I'm sure that most of us have at some point, committed the folly of instinctively associating someone's outward characteristics with our assessment of his inner nature.

A pleasing face is easily taken to contain a kind and loving soul while a gruffy face is often assumed to harbor a violent, dangerous or crude personality. Even the most learned and mature ones amongst us fall prey to this bias, and this becomes consequential when we act on such irrational beliefs, ending up with poor judgments and decisions. Teachers are guilty of this when they associate an outwardly well-behaved student with say being bright and hardworking. These preconceived notions may then unfairly reflect on the student's grades. In the workplace, the bias is likewise apparent, and seemingly accepted as well albeit not overtly. In employee appraisals, it is not uncommon that we come across instances where a single characteristic can be overly glorified, to the extent of lifting the entire evaluation that was meant to consider a myriad of other independent qualities. An employee may not have turned in a good performance, but from his sheer enthusiasm and pleasant demeanor, he may very well be given a better performance rating than what was rationally justifiable.

TV personality Carson Kressley said it best, *"People are much deeper than their stereotypes. That's the first place our minds go."* Only after we give time to hearing people's stories that we often go 'boy, I'd never have guessed'. We are easily led to wrongful conclusions about one's inner being from superficialities of his external form. To make matters worse, first impressions tend to stick. Often after we have seen someone first in a good light, it becomes difficult subsequently to darken that light, no matter the experience afterwards. Despite all good reason not to adopt such bias, it remains curiously persistent.

This bias is most brazenly exploited in marketing and advertising, playing right up to our impulses. It is no surprise that huge sums are poured into advertising just to steal a few moments from attractive celebrities who may well be endorsing products of little relevance to their trade, expertise or knowledge. It doesn't help that as consumers, we willingly subscribe to this manner of advertisement. We more or less lean on the false assurance that a good-looking person would also be honest and trustworthy.

This bias has much worse repercussions when it leads to malicious condemnation and discrimination. From telling our children that people with tattoos are not to be trusted, to associating fat people with laziness, these mindsets eventually form the basis of a toxic culture corrupted by bullying, rejection and alienation. *"If only our eyes saw souls instead of bodies, how very different our ideas of beauty would be."*

Technology to the Rescue

Identifying with our biases is a courageous first step towards guarding against them. Awareness always paves the way for positive action, be it in exercising greater self-control or taking corrective steps. The advent of technology has made our jobs easier in confronting our subconscious prejudices and correcting any naturally-occurring destructive tendencies.

For one, computers and software are 'emotionless' tools that will always fare better than us humans on impartiality. Through purposeful use of these tools, we are able to systematically remove human biases through deliberate design. A good example would be the relative neutrality of customer reviews on products or services found in online forums. These forums typically allow open access to pretty much anyone who wishes to drop a comment or feedback, thus achieving a wide dataset which improves the collective credibility of its contents. At the same time, most forums provide the option for personal identities to be kept hidden or intentionally vague. This advantageously bars readers from biased judgments based on irrelevant aspects such as external appearance or demeanor, which would otherwise be unavoidable in a face-to-face encounter. It is no wonder that many of us regard such forums more highly on credibility, despite their informal and at times anonymous nature. There are deeper and richer qualities that can sometimes be uncovered when we drop the visuals. Of course, online platforms suffer their fair share of problems such as the presence of ill-meaning scams and cheats. But for the large part, they provide more benefit to us by allowing us to bypass the demerits of the halo effect, in ways facilitated by the perks of technology.

Beware the Halo Effect

We should all strive to keep a vigilant eye on how we interpret what we see. There are many things that appear one way on the surface but turn out the opposite in substance. When it comes to ideas, every idea should be given a fair chance to stand on its own merits, regardless of who proposes it. A good idea is a good idea even if proposed by a poorly looking beggar on the street. A bad idea is a bad idea, even if suggested by a polished executive in his finest suit. And likewise when it comes to judgments on someone's character, the worst villains may well be dressed in a suit and tie and speak fluent language for all we know.

While it may convenience ourselves to simply paint others with a broad brush of 'good' or 'bad' from visual input alone, let us steer clear of this laziness. We are accountable to each other, and answerable for assessing every situation on its own terms based on a rational assessment of costs and outcomes. In the spirit of treating others with the same genuine respect that we wish for ourselves, let's endeavor to rein in on our mind's biases and resist unfair judgments of a person's inner being with irrelevant external attributes. Like Elton John wrote in his song "Understanding Women", *"Don't judge a picture by the frame. Every man is not the same."*

22

About Prisons

"It is said that no one truly knows a nation until one has been inside its jails. A nation should not be judged by how it treats its highest citizens, but its lowest ones," said Nelson Mandela. I think you've probably guessed where I might be going with this. I'm going to put it out there, I think incarceration is by and large, unnecessary and cruel. Yet, it is most carelessly and excessively practiced, in a way that is also terrifyingly accepted.

Putting someone behind bars is a severe imposition, and it is only right that it be given the most careful of considerations by the most mature of minds. Only when deemed to be absolutely necessary can we remotely justify applying such a means, and even then it should still be wielded with great compassion because any excessive use would simply be unjust and dare I say inhumane. While I understand some of the practical motivations and well-meaning intents behind a criminal justice system and the long-held practice of putting those guilty behind bars, I am deeply doubtful about whether the end indeed justifies the means in most cases, and whether the intended final objective is ever truly achieved.

We often comfort ourselves with the popular opinion that an honorable end may justify less honorable means. For a self-perceived 'greater cause', some sacrifices appear justified as we grant ourselves more leeway on 'lesser' methods. On this, I stand on the side that believes great ends cannot be attained by base means. To quote Wilhelm Reich, *"the end is the means by which you achieve it. Today's step is tomorrow's life. The meanness and inhumanity of the means make you mean and inhuman and make the end unattainable."* While imprisonment may set out to achieve many objectives in the name of serving justice, I believe that in most cases, it fares dismally at what it is meant to achieve.

If we keep the end in mind, and stock-take how we've been 'performing' in terms of ensuring safety and security, there is sadly little evidence that shows a positive correlation between keeping people locked up and a reduced crime rate, nor do the horrors of incarceration and its impoverished conditions do much to lessen chances of recidivism. In all honesty, we need to question if this practice is sustained out of convenience and precedence, more so than to arrive at the original intent of ensuring a safe environment with low crime rates.

"Human kindness has never weakened the stamina or softened the fiber of a free people. A nation does not have to be cruel to be tough." - Franklin D. Roosevelt

There are two principles that I find prerequisite to any discussion on serving justice. First is that good people sometimes make bad decisions, and this could be a result of being at the wrong place at the wrong time. While some people may indeed mess up and cause harm to others, that does not make them bad. We all know humans are imperfect and we are aware that most of us have made mistakes. When we look inwards towards ourselves at our fair share of wrongdoings, we may more compassionately notice our biases towards the errors of others, and become more acutely cognizant of the unwholesome thought that we are less fallible than those who seem most at fault. Second, we should understand that to change a person, we must first rehabilitate his thoughts about himself. This does not require prison walls nor cuffs. It is an organic process starting from within and meant to last a lifetime. If our true intent is to bring the fallen back onto the right path, it is our moral responsibility to guard against punishments that do nothing to rehabilitate nor shape one's thoughts for the better.

Injustice masquerading as justice is one of the most dangerous psychological smoke screens. It gives free reign to the foulest of imaginations, provides tacit approval for the most vindictive of motives, and only tends towards a self-perpetuating cycle under its own guise. The only breakpoint from this vicious loop lies in a disciplined practice of both universal love and magnanimous forgiveness. *"The more we ignore [love's] potential to bring greater balance and deeper meaning to human existence, the more likely we are to continue to define history as one long inglorious record of man's inhumanity to man,"* said Aberjhani, accomplished poet and author of "Encyclopedia of the Harlem Renaissance". Forgiveness is actually more about setting free the prisoner within ourselves, and putting an end to the vicious cycle of hate and vengeance. We are bigger than becoming the very people who hurt us, for isn't punishment simply justice for the unjust. Like Carl Jung, Swiss psychiatrist and early founder of analytical psychology, said, *"the healthy man does not torture others – generally it is the tortured who turn into torturers."*

The intellectuals amongst us may seek to approach this topic from the mind and not the heart. I do not think there is a case for imprisonment no matter how we argue it. People generally accept this practice easily due to a lack of knowledge and direct experience of incarceration itself, and a clouded mental association between punishment and greater social and moral intents. It may seem to most of us sat comfortably on the other side of the fence that there is nothing too terrible about being put behind bars. It appears to be unpleasant only from deprivation of typical pleasures and luxuries, and rather lack any additional inflictions of pain and suffering, as opposed to say harsher punishment methods like caning. From this perspective, societies feel little moral compunction to rethink incarceration, since it already appears to be one of the more humane methods of punishment available.

Unfortunately, most things are not as they seem. This is especially so for the worst things in life. It takes intentional effort to tear down the deceptions of surface impressions, and deeply perceive what may be carefully hidden. Before one assumes, one should learn the facts and enough of them. Ironically, imprisonment isn't something most of us would ever get to personally experience ourselves, or want to for that matter. However, seeking to understand from those who have, with sincerity and an open mind sounds like a decent first step.

In my free time, I enjoy hanging out with ex-convicts, one of my favorite company in fact. They are invariably able to shed light on the many oft-buried realities of life through their personal stories and hard-earned lessons. I always walk away with a deep appreciation towards them, for the enlightened perspective of the many sides that exist to every person and every story. My ex-convict friends always manage to relate the hardest lessons with such grace and humility that you would never imagine that they had once experienced the ugliest sides of humanity. I love how they never fail to leave me with so much more hope, compassion and softness than I found them.

Many of the ex-convicts I know are extremely down-to-earth and resilient beyond measure. Many of them are simply trying their hardest to turn over a new leaf, make an honest keep and rebuild their lives. I do not intend to generalize for all, but I can say that this rings true at least for many of those I have met. One of the most important lessons I have learnt from them is to always seek to understand before judging. We are often pressed to make quick decisions, rush our thought processes and at times, doing all this just to gain approval and admiration for our displays of lightning-speed intellects. Unfortunately, this does nothing to help us discern the difference between intellect and wisdom.

No matter how obvious something appears to be, one should always reserve discretion to hear the other side of the story. Succumbing to shortcuts and jumping to conclusions may be tempting, but the human spirit is too complex to be simplified this way, and way too worthy to be cheapened by any form of simplification. It takes courage to seek the whole truth and to persist in uncovering all sides. Above all, it takes quite some self-discipline to take control of our own thoughts and resist being led into fallacies by taking in only the information presented to us. It is human nature that we choose to tell only the version of the story that makes us look good, for *"until the lion learns how to write, every story will glorify the hunter"*. Hence the duty is ours to consider subtler nuances and multiple facets to single issues. Sometimes, the hidden stories may never be brought to light, and possibly intentionally so. Erring on the side of giving benefit of the doubt may result in one or two missed shots sometimes, but is still better than a perfect score of misfires.

Understanding The Full Story

When we allow ourselves to delve deeper into finding out the true motivations behind certain crimes, we may realize that oftentimes, the circumstances under which misdeeds were committed are ridden with so much complexity. We may even find that when we project the same situations on ourselves, we may have easily erred the same way. We are all quite similarly fallible to moments of irrationality, for aren't we all made up of both the heart and the mind. I don't believe crime ever begins as a natural human condition. Almost always, the backstories reveal circumstantial stresses and painful compromises that had to be made which all culminated in a spur-of-the-moment misstep that later proved costly.

We can all relate well to hot-headed moments, instances when we are so overwhelmed by emotion and blinded from reason. Even for most of us safely treading on the right side of the law, we are not immune to doing things without first playing out the full consequences of our actions in our head. Some crimes are ironically fueled by the most intense and deepest kind of love, integrity and loyalty you will ever find, so much so that when such virtues are taken to the extreme, they sadly lead to disasters instead. As expressed by Michel de Montaigne, one of the most significant philosophers of the French Renaissance, *"there is no man so good that if he placed all his actions and thoughts under the scrutiny of the laws, he would not deserve hanging ten times in his life"*. The circumstances under which a crime is committed may include a mix of being at the wrong place with the wrong company at the wrong time. The so-called criminals may, at the time of perpetration, just come out of a traumatic experience such as the death of a loved one, where the wounds still cut deep and the psyche still feels weak. A combination of unfavorable circumstances, raging emotions, and bad luck, can become such a potent cocktail that even the strongest of minds may fail to guard against. There are cases where an innocent man selflessly pleaded guilty to a crime he did not commit in order to protect the actual perpetrator, a loved one, from serving time. There exist other cases whereby one succumbs to crime only because of an impulse so strong to protect another from getting hurt. Rather ironically, it is often when love is deepest that actions can become most irrational and oftentimes at great expense of personal consideration.

Let's also not forget that laws are dead, they being a set of statutes created by men, to better manage society with a common reference for judgments to be passed with greater consistency. Our laws by and large spell absolutes, and this is clearly incongruent to how the natural world operates which is far from black and white. While I agree on the necessity of having a legal system, I am conscious that its objective is ultimately to help keep order in society and maintain a safe environment for all to live in. The practice of law is a live art, and the mere fact that we humans are the ones applying laws means that its practice will always be subject to some level of opinion and could never be perfect. Realizing the imperfection of any system and its practice, gives us the sensitivity and necessary compassion to adopt a more holistic approach.

Laws aside, let us also be mindful that there are many types of unkind and malicious acts that are not illegal per se, but are allowed to run free. Some of these misdemeanors may appear innocuous when looked at either singly or over a brief timeframe, but bear insidious repercussions that linger on and lead to worse consequences in the long run. We may be easily charmed by those dressed in fine suits or who take on respectable positions in the public eye. But some of these people may in actual fact, be more crooked than those clad in prison stripes, but are simply fortunate enough to be luckier or smarter in their approach. Personally, these individuals disgust me so much more than the overt criminals. I am not out to diss the righteous majority, but I would like to be intentional in considering all possibilities, especially those that do not occur intuitively to us, in hopes that the lenses through which we view the world and others remain as clear as possible.

Just like many of us, I have for the longest time been hustled away from those with troubled pasts or complicated histories, as my loved ones attempt to keep me away from the perceived negative association. This blissful ignorance only later turned into revelation when through my personal experiences and interactions, I learnt about the many untold sides of people's stories. In fact, it is typical to find these stories intentionally hidden, as publicity of any form would be seen as cheapening any remaining shred of honor behind some of those consequential actions. For me, one key takeaway is to always look deeper. While on the surface, someone may be convicted under the court of law, the true story behind a person's actions should be given a fair chance to be genuinely understood and heard before any hurtful judgments are made.

It is always with great sympathy and a heavy heart that I listen to the stories behind crimes, as I am always then reminded of how incredibly blessed I am. Blessed not in terms of having none of the same vulnerabilities and weaknesses of character, but blessed in terms of having made my fair share of mistakes but under luckier circumstances that allowed me to still stay on the right side of the law. I am also reminded of how blessed I am to have a safety net of loved ones who unfailingly offer their forgiveness and support during my moments of weakness which have helped stop me from falling further. Indeed, not everything is black and white. The true meaning of this statement runs deep. When we condemn a person for his wrongdoings, we are also indirectly focusing on only the worst parts of him, out of everything that he may have done prior including all the good. At the same time, we are subconsciously elevating ourselves to an imagined state of perfection, as we separate ourselves from the perceived crooks and feel 'qualified' enough to pass absolute judgments on them. Unfortunately, judgments do break people, sometimes irreparably. I think it is reasonable to not seek to tear each other apart.

"What a person shows to the world is only one tiny facet of the iceberg hidden from sight. And more often than not, it's lined with cracks and scars that go all the way to the foundation of their soul." – Sherrilyn Kenyon, best-selling writer and author of the "Dark Hunter" series

Retribution or Rehabilitation

"An eye for an eye makes the whole world blind," said Mahatma Gandhi. The maturity of a society is marked by how we treat the unwanted, undesirable and suffering amongst us. When it comes to dealing with our feelings and thoughts, we are not always as clear-headed as we think we are. Our hearts and minds sometimes lead us in opposite directions, and we are vulnerable to kidding ourselves into believing that we are solving certain problems with 'solutions' that actually misdirect us into creating more problems elsewhere, while leaving existing problems unsolved. When it comes to using imprisonment as punishment, we tread a fine line between satisfying our retributive impulses, and meeting the objectives we set out to achieve in the first place.

"Act in such a way that you treat humanity, whether in your own person or in the person of any other, never merely as a means to an end, but always at the same time as an

end." – German philosopher, Immanuel Kant. Some of us may argue that locking someone behind bars achieves social security, for it physically keeps someone deemed dangerous away from general population. While this is true, there needs to be a sensible balance between maintaining security while still respecting the basic freedom of an individual whether he is a criminal or not. And by that, I mean according a just sentence that is commensurate with the severity of crime committed. There is good reason why security is usually managed with a multi-pronged approach. Other than keeping criminals in prisons, we have our policemen on patrol, community watch groups and surveillance presence. All these together help make the overall approach more balanced on all fronts. However, I find the particular measure of imprisonment has now become too easily triggered, since it conveniently rides on the widespread acceptance that it already enjoys as a form of punishment. The moral courage to attempt other possibly more appropriate options is difficult to muster.

Consider those convicted of crimes with little link to violence or danger, such as embezzlement or defamation. Sentencing those guilty of such crimes to imprisonment appears to achieve little in terms of security benefit. Or in instances involving very young offenders, incarceration is likely to do more harm than good. Not all cases require a period behind bars to achieve sentencing objectives.

It has been shown in studies that it is not so much the severity of punishment but the certainty of punishment that deters people from committing wrongdoings. We tout imprisonment as one of the better ways to intimidate people out of repeat offences, as it is seemingly harsher than a fine, but more humane than other draconian methods like caning and even execution. But simply because something is not 'bad enough' does not make it good enough. In our subconscious, we are usually just cherry-picking our benchmarks to convince ourselves of what we already wanted to believe at the outset. Does imprisonment serve to benefit both the convicted and society at large in terms of the bigger intent of ensuring a safer environment? If we break it down, I find arguments for incarceration actually mostly weak.

Above all else, I do not subscribe to using intimidation to subdue another. To me, any approach that uses force on another in a humiliating manner is wrong, period. If we put aside our urge for vengeance, and choose to understand that what's done cannot be undone and what can only be changed is in the here and now, then perhaps we can think clearer. The conditions of most prisons today, think extended periods of isolation, stale air, poor hygiene, and austere controls on your daily activities to name a few, are more than sufficient to make a normal person go crazy, not to mention those who already started off broken.

Despite all this, most of us appear satisfied with or perhaps choose to remain apathetic about the current state of affairs. It is with false optimism that we still think that those who have gone through extended periods of imprisonment, where they are stripped of basic dignity and self-respect, and have had to suffer tremendous emotional stress and isolation, will be able to come out as better versions of themselves. While there are some well-managed prisons in some parts of the world, such as in Norway, these are sadly few and far between. It doesn't take a genius to figure that the very circumstances of prison provide the worst environment for any rehabilitation. Instead, I daresay it would be a miracle if these criminals did not take a turn for the worse and become ever more disillusioned about humanity, and in some cases, harbor further criminal thoughts to seek vengeance for the suffering they have been put through. With few role models or support systems to lean on, any sliver of hope to change for the better is honestly quite a tall order. Yet, many of us do naively expect the incarcerated to turn over a new leaf upon their release, and even go as far as to give credit to the prison sentence as a praiseworthy game-changer in effecting any positive transformation. Unfortunately, in all honesty, it is difficult to get back on track when you are ostracized and rejected, with little to no guidance and support. It is no wonder that most criminals fall into a perpetuating cycle of crime, as it sometimes seems like the only way for them to survive.

At the end of the day, I believe that all pain is bad, including the pain of the wrongdoer. Inflicting harm should only be considered if it achieves a greater cause of preventing something worse. Otherwise, retribution for its own sake can never justify its ills. Call me naïve, but I believe the only sensible response when someone hurts you is to love him back. The choice to do better than the poorly treatment you received, is tough but never a wrong one.

A Little Benefit Of Doubt Goes A Long Way

Any system created by men carries inherent imperfections, and any system operated by men will carry its fair share of failings. There is much that we do not see and hear about; we often know too little to judge. Hence leaving some benefit of the doubt often goes a long way.

The odds are usually stacked against the prosecuted, it is not difficult to see why. It would be naïve to imagine any justice system could achieve a perfectly level playing field, especially within the constraints of laws and their limited methods of application. For one, circumstantial evidence that is considered for some cases, may sometimes place an impossible task on the innocent for proving they are not guilty beyond reasonable doubt. It is worth knowing that circumstantial evidence is not direct evidence, such as an eyewitness' testimony, but is instead indirect evidence that provides leeway for prosecutors to 'design' allegations. These allegations could be specifically designed to convince a jury that the defendant is guilty, by implying that something happened instead of by directly proving so. And of course, we all know that the jury isn't perfect, they being a group of people just like you and me, with imperfect knowledge of all relevant facts and carrying their own unique biases. Yet, for the individual fighting for his innocence, his entire life would literally be hanging by a thread and at the mercy of these clockwork judicial processes. All professions however noble, will not be immune to their fair share of 'black sheep'. In some cases, some of the biggest villains may be the lawyers themselves, when selfish gains override better judgment.

There are also other times when outcomes can vary hugely under the same set of laws but applied in different cultural contexts. For instance, in the use of 'sudden provocation' as defense, what is defined as sufficiently provocative is directly related to how conservative a society is. In this regard, the same laws may therefore be applied with varying degrees of consideration. For example, in the practice of a mandatory death sentence, some societies may respect the individual's right to a proper defense more than others and hence accord varying extents of assistance, such as where financial help is needed to engage a lawyer.

While I do not expect those who hold judicial positions to possess the kind of omniscience to carry out their duties with godly precision, I think we could minimally manage flexibility in approach. At the end of the day, we should minimally recognize that there is no perfect fit between a criminal justice system and justice itself. The allowance for this gap in our minds would at least allow some compassion and understanding to enter. It is also worthwhile to remain sensitive to the limitations of our own knowledge, and suspend judgment when there is slightest ambivalence on the whole truth. As W.H. Auden said, *"Under the look of fatigue, the attack of migraine and the sigh. There is always another story."*

Final Thoughts

"To forgive is to set a prisoner free and discover that the prisoner was you," - Lewis Smedes, renowned Christian author and theologian in the Reformed tradition. I am certainly not attempting, in this chapter, to suggest that we should all go as far as to reward those who have committed offences. But I do appeal for them to be treated respectfully, no less than how you and me would like to be treated if we were in their shoes. Yes some of us

have made mistakes, some of which are undeniably grave errors. However, that does not change the fact that the past stays in the past. The best way forward is only from a place of kindness, forgiveness and compassion, if what we are truly after is to crush all remaining seeds of hate, malice and vengeance.

Acknowledgements

There are so many people I'd like to thank, some of whom may not get to read this, but nonetheless the thanks goes out anyway.

I have been tremendously blessed with opportunities to meet wonderful people, often under the most random and unintended of circumstances. So many unbelievable life stories have been exchanged and so many lessons I have learnt from these people.

Some of my acquaintances became fleeting loves, others remain till this day as my silent but solid rocks of support. If you know me personally, you would understand how I love easily, and how I love everyone. Every friend is kin to me, dressed in the simplest clothing or covered in tattoos, these don't matter to me.

There is someone special I couldn't not mention, one of the smartest people I know and my favorite Arian by far. Thank you for being the best support I could wish for when I was at a pretty weak place. Naming you may embarrass you, so I will avoid doing so and err on the conservative side if I have to. Because no one can beat your supernatural smarts, you will know who you are anyway. Just know that I'm always grateful to how you offered your time, probably one of your most prized possessions knowing the million and one things you are busy with, and for your most genuine company even though I was just an inconsequential stranger who couldn't offer anything in return. Your wise words did jolt me and eventually led to some reorganizations in my life that were for the better, something that rarely happens to be honest. I know I'm combative in spirit and borderline obsessed about certain things, but that in no way dims the gratitude I feel towards your generosity and honesty.

Thank you Brendan, someone I have known for more than two decades and actually miraculously still on my phone's contact list. I am terrible at keeping in touch with people in general, so nothing short of a blessing to still have you close, as one of my go-to friends whenever I find myself needing some comfortable company.

Thank you to so many of my silent guardian angels. That unwavering support has honestly been so great that I often think I don't quite deserve it or have reciprocated enough. Each and every one of you is so incredibly special to me, and I hope you all know how much I appreciate all of that support and concern, including whatever's left unspoken. Thank you Pin Yun, Serene, Sam, Yvonne, Jade, Aunty Beatrice, Kim Chuan, Roland, Fabian, Alvin, Francis, Chee How, Alex, Dr Tay, Cassian and so many more I have unintentionally missed mentioning or have painfully refrained from including here for fear of turning this into a parody of an overrun Hollywood thank-you speech. Just know in my heart I appreciate all of you whom I've crossed paths with who have directly or indirectly, outwardly or silently backed my endeavors and dreams.

Thanks to my family, especially my parents, for their unfailing tolerance, ever-patient love and first-class care. Even though they may not always know or understand what I was exactly up to, and have also had to put up with the strange silences I slip into for days on end, their faith in me has never once wavered. I can only say that I will always be tremendously grateful for that unconditional belief and trust, despite the very little I share and the very little I can express well enough in words when I do share.

And of course, last but definitely not least, thanks to the whole team at Partridge without which this book would never see the light of day. My heartfelt thanks goes out to each and every one of you who have contributed one way or another to the publishing process, including those who have worked hard behind the scenes and whom I may not know personally. Thank you so much.

Notes

1. About Tenderness

1 Alan W. Watts, *The Wisdom of Insecurity: A Message for an Age of Anxiety*
2 Eric Hanson, *thepoeticunderground: Stars (pg 81)*
3 John Rawls, *A Theory of Justice*
4 Plutarch, *The Parallel Lives, The life of Solon*

2. About Love

1 Mary Ruefle, *Madness, Rack and Honey*
2 Mother Teresa, *Mother Teresa*

3. About Authenticity

1 Adam Grant, *Unless You're Oprah, 'Be Yourself' is Terrible Advice (New York Times)*
2 Dr. CA Vishnu Bharath Alampali, *LIFE IS LIKE A JOURNEY ON A TRAIN: WHAT IS LIFE*
3 Brene Brown, *The Gifts of Imperfection: Let Go of Who You Think You're Supposed to Be and Embrace Who You Are*
4 Victoria Erickson, *http://hopemovementau.tumblr.com/post/115440794547/life-is-too-short-for-pretend-dont-do-things-by*

4.   About Everyday People

1   Students' Academy, *Words of Wisdom: John F. Kennedy*

2   Lincoln Konkle, *Thornton Wilder and the Puritan Narrative Tradition*

3   Tina Williamson, *How Kindness will Change your Life and the World*, https://www.huffingtonpost.com/tina-williamson/how-kindness-will-change- b 5009651.html

5.   About Identity

1   Sadashivan Nair, *Who Am I, Why Am I, I Don't Know*

2   John Locke, *An Essay Concerning Human Understanding*

3   Ming D. Liu, *Who am I, you ask?* http://mingdliu.com/post/95400126012/who-am-i-you-ask-i-am-made-from-all-the-people

6.   About Art

1   Osho, *The Book of Wisdom - The Heart of Tibetan Buddhism*

2   John Steinbeck, *Travels with Charley: In Search of America*

3   Ananda Coomaraswamy, *The Wisdom of Ananda Coomaraswamy*

4   Kathy Coffey, *The Art of Faith*

5   Rupi Kaur, *Milk and Honey*

7. About Courage

1 Harper Lee, *To Kill A Mockingbird*
2 Osho, *Courage: The Joy of Living Dangerously*

8. About Independent Thought

1 C.S. Lewis, *Image and Imagination*
2 Amol H. Kandekar, *Poems of Peace Pleasure Dreams: Sweet Lovely Poems*
3 Brad Schreiber, *What are You Laughing At?*
4 Malik S. Muhammad, *Think Big, Grow Big, In Business and In Life!*

9. About Productivity

1 Stephen R. Covey, *The Seven Habits of Highly Effective People*
2 Robin Sharma, *The Greatness Guide*
3 P.S. Satish, *Knowing Is Not Same as Doing*

10. About Small Talk

1 Sakyong Mipham, *The Lost Art of Good Conversation: A Mindful Way to Connect with Others and Enrich Everyday Life*
2 Oscar Wilde, *De Profundis: The Ballad of Reading Gaol and Other Writings*
3 Gagan Madan, *Everyone Has a Right to Love*
4 Quote by AVA, *https://www.pinterest.co.uk/pin/317222367484828533/ (Dana Hillestad)*

11.   About Existentialism

1   Richard O. Brooks, *Plato and Modern Law*

2   Glyn Hughes, *Squashed Philosophers*

3   William Shakespeare, Thomas Price, *The Wisdom and Genius of Shakespeare*

4   Soren Kierkegaard, *Either/Or: A Fragment of Life*

12.   About Engagement

1   Mihaly Csikszentmihalyi, *Flow: The Psychology of Optimal Experience*

2   George Carlin, *Brain Droppings*

3   Walt Whitman, *Song of Myself*

4   John Medina, *Brain Rules: 12 Principles for Surviving and Thriving at Work, Home and School*

5   Viktor Frankl, *Man's Search for Meaning*

13.   About Tolerance

1   G.K. Chesterton, *On Lying in Bed and Other Essays*

2   Mother Teresa, *The Joy in Loving: A Guide to Daily Living*

3   Audre Lorde, *Sister Outsider: Essays and Speeches*

4   Ian Moore, *Unpossible Thinking*

5   Jean Paul Sartre, *Nausea*

6   Nikita Gill, *People Survive in Different Ways*

14.   About Women

1   Pam Reinke, *Wild Women Creed*

2   Nikita Gill, *The Ghost of All The Women, How to Love Someone Who Is Broken*

15. About Food

1 Harriet Van Horne, *Vogue (1956)*
2 Sadhguru, *Repair your body from inside (May 2017), https://www.youtube.com/ watch?v=-4b5G544xa0*
3 Alex Atala, *Chef's Table (May 2016), https://www. youtube.com/watch?v=op3YmluuAN0*
4 Thomas Keller, *The French Laundry Cookbook*
5 Jim McGrody, *What We Feed Our Patients*

16. About Solitude

1 Johann Wolfgang von Goethe, *The Sorrows of Young Werther; Elective Affinities; Novella*
2 Rainer Maria Rilke, *Letters to a Young Poet*
3 William Shakespeare, *Hamlet*
4 Anthony Storr, *Solitude – A Return to Self*
5 Peter H. Thomas, *Be Great: The Five Foundations of an Extraordinary Life in Business - and Beyond*
6 Elle Harrison, *Wild Courage: A journey of transformation for you and your business*
7 Tao Yuan Ming, *On Drinking Wine*

17. About Friendships

1 Aristotle, *The Essential Aristotle*
2 Joseph Epstein, *Friendship:An Expose*
3 C.S. Lewis, *The Four Loves*
4 Plato, *The Republic*
5 William L. Randall, Elizabeth McKim, *Reading our Lives: The Poetics of Growing Old*
6 Søren Kierkegaard, *Either/Or*
7 Erich Fromm, *The Art of Loving*

18.   About Special Occasions

1   Mitch Albom, *Tuesdays with Morrie*
2   Anne Frank, *The Diary of Anne Frank*

19.   About Education

1   Melanie Young, *Follow Your Dreams*
2   Matt Cohen, Wayne Grady, *The Quebec Anthology, 1830-1990*
3   Janie Victoria Ward, *The Skin We're In*
4   Joseph Agassi, *The Hazard Called Education*
5   Edmund Burke, *Selected Letters of Edmund Burke*
6   Aristotle, *Aristotle on Education: Extracts from the Ethics and Politics*
7   Michel de Montaigne, *The Complete Essays*
8   Bill Bullard, *"For the Faculty", Commencement 2007, San Francisco University High School*
9   Ronald Arthur Howard, Clinton D. Korver, *Ethics for the Real World*
10   E. Christopher Reyes, *In His Name*
11   Karl Popper, *Conjectures and Refutations: The Growth of Scientific Knowledge*
12   Anthony Clare, *On Men: Masculinity in Crisis*
13   Judith Groch, *The Right to Create*
14   Will Richardson, *From Master Teacher to Master Learner*
15   John Medina, *Brain Rules*

20.   About Death

1   Lao Tzu, *Tao Te Ching (Verse 29)*
2   Mitch Albom, *Tuesdays with Morrie*
3   Seneca, *On the Shortness of Life*

21. About Appearance

22. About Prisons

7   Michel de Montaigne, *The Complete Essays*
8   Ramnarine Sahadeo, *Mohandas K. Gandhi: Thoughts, Words, Deeds*
9   Immanuel Kant, *Groundwork of the Metaphysics of Morals*
10 W.H. Auden, *At Last the Secret is Out*
11 Lewis B. Smedes, *Forgive and Forget: Healing the Hurts We Don't Deserve*

Printed in the United States
By Bookmasters